Practical Counseling Tools for Pastoral Workers

by

Dr. Dan Montgomery

Pauline

BOOKS & MEDIA

BOSTON

Library of Congress Cataloging-in-Publication Data

Montgomery, Dan, 1946-
    Practical counseling tools for pastoral workers / Dan Montgomery.
        p.   cm.
    ISBN 0-8198-5899-4 (paper)
    1. Pastoral counseling. 2. Peer counseling in the church.
3. Church work—Catholic Church. 4. Catholic Church—Membership.
    I. Title.
    BV4012.2.M57   1996
    253.5—dc20   96-1948
                                                    CIP

Cover photo: Mary Emmanuel Alves, FSP

Printed and published in the U.S.A. by Pauline Books & Media, 50 St. Paul's Avenue, Boston, MA 02130.

Pauline Books & Media is the publishing house of the Daughters of St. Paul, an international congregation of women religious serving the Church with the communications media.

1 2 3 4   99 98 97 96

To Katie,
my beloved wife and editor,
who stands by my side in all I do.

And to
The Daughters of St. Paul,
for their enthusiastic support.

About the Author

Dr. Dan Montgomery is a licensed clinical psychologist with 25,000 hours of counseling experience. He is the author of *God and Your Personality* and *Beauty in the Stone: How God Sculpts You into the Image of Christ*. In addition to his private practice, he has taught in four universities, holding advanced degrees in psychology and philosophy.

An internationally known conference speaker, Dr. Montgomery is committed to an extensive speaking schedule and is available for a variety of organizations. His magazine articles are read by 30 million people worldwide and have appeared in publications that include *Catholic Digest, The Priest, Eucharistic Minister, Pastoral Life, Messenger of St. Anthony, Catholic Parent* and *Guideposts*.

Dr. Montgomery may be contacted by writing:

681 Portofino Lane
Foster City, CA 94404
415-354-8018

Contents

One

Compass Counseling

J esus Christ initiates the great revolution—the redemption and transformation of one's soul and personality—whenever he enters a human heart. "I came that they may have life," he said, "and have it abundantly" (John 10:10). One's feelings, thoughts and behavior come under the influence of the Master teacher of interior prayer, the Holy Spirit.

The principles of counseling can augment the ministries of pastoral workers in their missions of soul healing, personality clarification and reconciling people to one another. Counseling can integrate the presence of the loving Christ and the power of the Holy Spirit with the process of becoming a whole person.

I first became interested in counseling while I was teaching philosophy courses in a seminary. I felt touched by the human needs of my students and wanted to offer them something more than insight into philosophy and religion. I looked for tools that could promote self-understanding and help them experience intimacy with God and others.

My search for practical people-helping tools led me out of the seminary and into the field of clinical psychology. There

I learned the principles and techniques of counseling. Through years of private practice I have seen how the development of a healthy personality brings a person closer to God and others. I've taught the principles and techniques of counseling to graduate students, mental health counselors and pastoral workers. In religious life, these principles can be applied in one-on-one or group counseling sessions, therapeutic preaching, spiritual direction or religious education.

Compass Counseling

Compass counseling—the approach to Christian counseling and pastoral work that I have pioneered—combines the knowledge of psychology with that of human nature revealed through the Word of God.

Compass counseling takes into account valuable insights from the psychologists of the twentieth century, several of whom I have personally worked with. These insights include:

• the depth psychology of Sigmund Freud, Carl Jung and Karen Horney, which describes the ego defense mechanisms that block human growth;

• the existential psychology of Viktor Frankl, Rollo May and Adrian van Kaam, which emphasizes self-responsibility and the freedom to choose;

• the height psychology of Abraham Maslow, Carl Rogers and Everett Shostrom, which affirms the uniqueness of every person.

Yet, the central focus of compass counseling remains the galvanizing presence of the Father, Son and Holy Spirit in personality and counseling. Jesus Christ's personality is the model for understanding the principles of a healthy—or balanced—personality.

Priest-psychologist Adrian van Kaam writes:

The source of Christian spirituality is the Lord; he is our spiritual Master *par excellence.* He gently guides his followers through his Church, through Scripture, and through his Holy Spirit speaking in their hearts.[1]

Have you ever considered that the names of Christ reveal important aspects of his personality? Four names in particular reveal his inner compass—a compass of the self. Just as a physical compass has four points to guide in the right direction, so the compass of the self has four compass points—*love, assertion, weakness* and *strength*—that epitomize Christ's balanced personality.

The Rose of Sharon captures Christ's *love* compass point. His love is incredibly pure. He forgives our faults and reaches out with a helping hand. "Indeed, God did not send the Son into the world to condemn the world, but in order that the world might be saved through him" (John 3:17). Jesus is a lover of the human soul, the original and everlasting Good Samaritan.

Remember the woman who was about to be stoned to death for adultery? She looked through a veil of tears and saw Jesus. His compassion bathed her emotional wounds. He forgave her sins and offered her a new life. She left the stoning place unharmed, with God's love infusing her being.

But Christ wasn't tender in every situation, or else he would have bent over backward to please everyone. His love compass point was balanced by his *assertion,* or righteous indignation. The name Lion of Judah expresses Christ's assertion compass point. A fierce opponent of injustice, Christ stood up for the poor and the meek.

Jesus drove the moneychangers out of his Father's temple. He rebuked evildoers and challenged self-righteous Pharisees. "But woe to you Pharisees! For you tithe mint and rue and herbs of all kinds, and neglect justice and the love of God" (Luke 11:42). And Jesus confronted the devil. "Away with you Satan! For it is written, worship the Lord your God, and serve only him" (Matthew 4:8).

But love and assertion fall short of describing Christ's complete personality. The Lamb of God—the symbol of his redemptive mission—shows his vulnerability. How did the Son of God experience the *weakness* compass point? Jesus shuddered with fear and dread in the Garden of Gethsemane, foreseeing the horror of the cross. During his crucifixion, he yelled out, "Father, why have you forsaken me?" Through weakness he became a living sacrifice for our sins. "For he was crucified in weakness, but lives by the power of God" (2 Corinthians 13:4).

Jesus died in his weakness only to be raised from the dead as the Prince of Peace—his strength compass point. The Father placed him in authority over all creation. "Authority rests upon his shoulders: and he is named Wonderful Counselor, Mighty God, Everlasting Father, Prince of Peace" (Isaiah 9:6).

Because of Christ's personality balance, his eternal power is the strength of a loving servant, not the militant rule of a despot. His strength is tempered by love, assertion and weakness.

Jesus—the Son of God and the Son of Man—is a marvelously balanced personality. He calls us, with the Holy Spirit's help, to develop a similar balance in ourselves. In Christ we find the true and living ground for counseling, pastoral work and inspired lay leadership.

Compass Counseling and Spiritual Shepherding

Compass counseling helps pastoral workers to heal personality conflicts, resolve power struggles and reconcile personality clashes. When psychological wounds are healed, spiritual communion can be restored.

If the congregation has members who are too dependent,

too aggressive, too withdrawn or too controlling, compass principles can guide them toward Christlike wholeness. Compass counseling empowers the laity as well. Talented lay leaders have vital gifts for enriching the body of Christ. Vatican II strongly encourages the participation of lay leaders in parish ministries. "The laity," says the new *Catechism*, "dedicated as they are to Christ and anointed by the Holy Spirit, are marvelously called and prepared so that even richer fruits of the Spirit may be produced in them."[2]

Spiritual shepherding—whether by clergy or lay leaders is complex and demanding, a varied mixture of psychology and spirituality that brings together the redemptive power of Christ and everyday coping.

Eugene Peterson, himself a pastor for thirty years, writes of the Church:

> Her theology can be profound, her meditations mystic, her moral counsels wise, her liturgies splendid. But until she is dragged into the common round she is not alive with the Good News nor does she have a chance to put her ideas and beliefs to use, testing them out in actual life-situations.
>
> Pastoral work is...the pragmatic application of religion in the present.[3]

As in Jesus' own ministry, spiritual shepherds need to integrate the eternal word of God with the particular needs of people. This book gives pastoral workers practical tools for:

• modeling their own personality on our Lord's life and personality;

• understanding and transforming people's personality patterns when these are incompatible with an abundant life;

• handling troublesome emotions such as anger, guilt or depression—in a counseling session;

- turning parishioners' feelings of inferiority or superiority into graced self-acceptance;
- helping people develop an intimate trust in the Father, Son and Holy Spirit;
- building effective and diplomatic relationships with others;
- actualizing the virtues of compassion, courage, humility and dignity.

In my early years of counseling, I often felt confused about how to build rapport with people and help them grow in Christ. In developing the fundamentals and techniques of compass counseling, I've learned how to assess people's difficulties in a first session, and generate practical growth stretches that facilitate personality balance in the sessions that follow.

Here is my prayer for you, dear reader: "May the Father bless your calling as a pastoral worker. May the Lord Jesus enhance your people-helping skills and increase your personality balance. And may the Holy Spirit anoint you for helping others find personality health and wholeness. In Jesus' name. Amen."

Two

The Compass of the Self

To live a spiritual life, writes Henri Nouwen, "means first of all to come to the awareness of the inner polarities between which we are held in tension."[4] Compass counseling helps people experience and express the universal polarities of personality known as love, assertion, weakness and strength.

Love is the glue in relationships which provides interest, attraction, tenderness and compassion. Through his love, God approaches humanity through his Son Jesus Christ. "For God so loved the world that he gave his only Son, so that everyone who believes in him may not perish, but may have eternal life" (John 3:16).

Through love, people approach God heart to heart. Jesus said, "You shall love the Lord your God with all your heart, and with all your soul, and with all your mind" (Matthew 22:37).

Counselees may have had their love compass point damaged as a result of traumatic or dysfunctional relationships. When people are betrayed, abused or disillusioned, they pull back from the love compass point for fear of being hurt again. Counseling can heal the wounds of a broken heart and impart the courage to love again—this time with greater discernment and personality balance.

Assertion enables people to express feelings, confront injustice and experience the courage to follow Christ. Through assertion, people approach God with boldness. "Let us therefore approach the throne of grace with boldness" (Hebrews 4:16). Assertion is also needed to face the hardships that life brings. Jesus said, "In the world you shall have tribulation" (John 16:33, KJV).

Counselees need to awaken the assertion compass point in order to face their deepest feelings and grow in the valley of pain. They may have to take stands against people or events responsible for undue suffering. Compass counseling shows them how to be assertive, not aggressive—how to diplomatically express feelings and needs while respecting the rights of others.

Through *weakness*, people confess their sins to God. "If we confess our sins, he who is faithful and just will forgive us our sins and cleanse us from all unrighteousness" (1 John 1:9). People benefit from talking over their shortcomings with one another or with a pastoral worker. In the sacrament of Reconciliation, Catholics receive the gift of complete forgiveness of sins, along with healing grace to avoid sin in the future. "Therefore confess your sins to one another, and pray for one another, so that you may be healed" (James 5:16).

Healthy weakness allows people to discuss their faults and failures without feeling humiliated. When counselees experience that their self-disclosure doesn't result in condemnation, they grasp that anything human is worthy of understanding. They can learn from failures and let go of regrets.

When counselees surrender to the weakness compass point they acquire teachable spirits. They find themselves strengthened by the act of reaching out. St. Paul wrote that "power is made perfect in weakness" (2 Corinthians 12:9).

Healthy weakness provides the continuing opportunity for personality transformation. *Strength* reflects self-worth and fosters adequacy, competence and identity. Through strength, people approach God confidently as their heavenly Father. "So let us not grow weary in doing what is right, for we will reap at harvest time, if we do not give up" (Galatians 6:9). Through strength, God does for people what they cannot do for themselves. "For nothing will be impossible with God" (Luke 1:37).

As counselees find their way toward personality balance, they are confident and *strong*, yet humbly aware of *weakness* and need. They can express *love* and forgiveness to others or use diplomatic *assertion* to stand against unfairness. Balanced, well-rounded people maintain free and equal access to all four compass points of the inner personality compass.

The Compass of the Self

If the self is symbolized as a circle, then we can picture two polarities crisscrossing at the center of a person's compass. In compass counseling, these poles, or *compass points*, are called the Love–Assertion polarity, and the Weakness–Strength polarity. Taking the first letter of each pole, these reference points can be remembered as the LAWS of personality and relationships.

Using Jesus as our model for personality health, the four points around the perimeter act as inner guides.

This compass of the self is a pastoral tool that helps people find bearings within themselves and in relation to other people. They develop Christlike personalities by learning to use all four compass points. The image of God can shine through them.

I usually explain to counselees in a first session that most difficulties in life—family problems, emotional confusion,

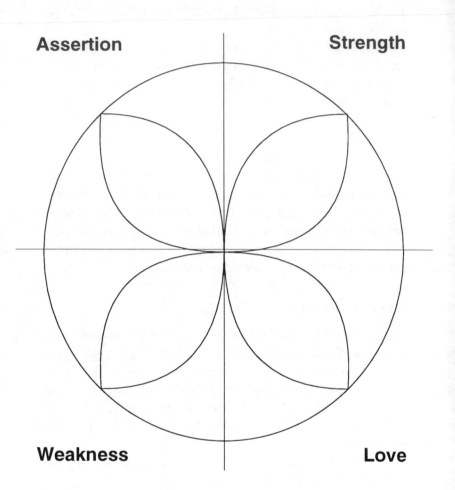

The Compass of the Self

addiction, sexual dysfunction or spiritual quandaries—spring from one's personality pattern. Too often counselees believe that other people are responsible for their difficulties when the real conflicts are within themselves.

I show counselees a picture of the compass of the self and explain the function of each compass point. I ask how their behavior stacks up. They discover which of the compass points they avoid and which ones they exaggerate. By taking active steps toward personality balance—called growth stretches or homework—counselees take responsibility for their psychological and spiritual growth in Christ.

By the end of a first or second session counselees often report a sense of relief. Then they feel better prepared to begin their journey of growth and healing. One man said, "Finding out where I am helps me know that I can change."

When educating people about the compass of the self, encourage them to talk openly about how they have behaved in the past and present. Explain that rigid behaviors are out of balance and self-defeating. The honest recognition of self-defeating patterns is essential to therapeutic progress.

Rhythm versus Rigidity

Imagine a skater gracefully cutting the ice in figure-eights and you can picture the rhythmic swings between the compass points that mark a fully-functioning personality. Love isn't better than assertion and strength isn't better than weakness. Each polarity or compass point handles certain life situations and each was demonstrated in the life of our Lord.

A flexible rhythm of behavior brings out a person's originality and creativity. These swings can be small arcs of lesser intensity or larger swings of greater intensity. Saying "I care about you" to someone is less intense than saying "I love you deeply." Saying "I feel irritated" is less intense than saying "I'm terribly angry at you."

Mini-swings of expression are generally preferred in human communication because they can be more relaxed and diplomatic. However, some occasions seem to require maxi-swings of expression, as when our Lord overturned tables and threw the moneychangers out of his Father's temple.

It is important for counselees to learn how to suppress as well as to express themselves. At times it is wiser to hold back one's opinions or feelings in order to express them at a better time and place. However, if self-expression is repressed, or pushed out of conscious awareness, then inner pressures build up which skew one's personality. When repression is involved, rigid behavior replaces rhythmic, creative living.

Personality health is attained by integrating and coordinating love and assertion, weakness and strength, in the service of the spiritual core, to which we now turn our attention.

The Spiritual Core

The spiritual core—the center of our being—is the source of a counselee's God-given personhood. The spiritual core reflects the fact that he or she is made in the image of God and has an intimate relationship with him. Jesus said, "Behold, the kingdom of God is within you" (Luke 17:21). The Holy Spirit dwells within the core and inspires our counselees to become more Christlike.

Richard McBrien, Chairman of the Department of Theology at the University of Notre Dame, writes:

"This Kingdom, of course, is available to every human being as 'grace and mercy,' and yet each individual gains entrance through a total interior renewal which the Gospel calls *metanoia*; it is a radical conversion, a profound change of mind and heart."[5]

Compass counseling facilitates this inner metanoia by freeing counselees from inner conflicts, smoothing out their relationships, and deepening their trust in God. The Holy Spirit plays a vital role in counseling and pastoral work.

Jesus said: "As the Scripture has said, 'Out of the believer's heart shall flow rivers of living water.' Now he said that about the Spirit, which believers in him were to receive" (John 7:38-39).

Many counselees respond positively to the artesian well model for understanding the presence of the Holy Spirit within the personality. An artesian well is made by boring deep into the earth until water is reached. By the force of internal pressure, the water then gushes up like a fountain. The source of the water is always higher up, from the top of a hill or mountain.

From this high point, the water seeps down underneath the earth and converges into a mighty stream. By drilling the well deep enough for its bottom to fall out, the core of the well connects to an underground reservoir of water. The force of nature pushes the water from the underground river up through the core of the well. An abundance of water becomes available at the surface of the artesian well. The well keeps flowing as long as its core stays clean and open.

Father van Kaam writes: "We will see in eternal gratefulness how the inner spring of grace made our deepest self similar to Jesus. We will see how the spring inside us leaps up with dazzling splendor for all eternity."[6]

Pastoral workers and counselors can call upon the Holy Spirit to guide the therapeutic process. God's presence in the counseling process helps form a therapeutic alliance with counselees that encourages inner renewal and promotes personality growth.

Trusting the Holy Spirit means receiving God's power to counsel others in a caring and balanced way. The Holy Spirit helps counselors and counselees alike to give up worry, fears and false pride.

What I refer to as the spiritual core, Scripture refers to as the heart. The word "heart" is used in Scripture to designate the seat of life—it means one's entire nature and understanding. Counselees need to discover these important aspects of the spiritual core:

• trust in the Inner Supreme Court—their inner truth in Christ—for decision-making. "My sheep hear my voice. I know them, and they follow me" (John 10:27);

• the ability to use intelligence in open-minded and unbiased ways. "Trust in the Lord with all your heart, and do not rely on your own insight...do not be wise in your own eyes" (Proverbs 3:5, 7);

• courage to grow as a person-in-process—by the grace of God. "But grow in the grace and knowledge of our Lord and Savior Jesus Christ" (2 Peter 3:18);

• trust in the heart's desires, knowing that these often correspond with God's will. "Take delight in the Lord, and he will give you the desires of your heart" (Psalm 37:4);

• an inner attitude of prayer and trust in the Holy Spirit. "But the Advocate, the Holy Spirit, whom the Father will send in my name, will teach you every-thing, and remind you of all that I have said to you" (John 14:26).

One of the paradoxes of personal growth is that it can never be forced. We need to be patient with ourselves and our counselees. Every person must grow at his or her own pace, in the wisdom of God.

None of us lives from the spiritual core all the time, or perhaps even most of the time. Sin and self-will taint all of us. Growth toward authentic personhood does not happen automatically, because rigid patterns of personality are not easily dismantled. Our counselees cannot change suddenly even if they want to.

Patience with the growth process and surrender to the grace of God are essential for being a person-in-process. Lasting change involves a gradual, steady process of becoming.

The Holy Spirit is our lead partner in the ministries of counseling and pastoral work.

Three

Compass Counseling in Action

Greg and Kathryn attended an Ivy League university together. Greg had handsome features and athletic prowess. A petite young woman, Kathryn's intelligence matched her charm. Friends described them as the perfect couple. They attended the same church on Sundays, and sometimes prayed together. After a year of dating, they began talking over the possibility of marriage.

One afternoon Greg came to Kathryn's apartment. He sat down close to her on the sofa and then demanded, "Take off your clothes."

"What?" she asked.

"I mean it. We've gone steady for a year and it's time to make love. You'll like it. Now get undressed."

Kathryn felt stunned and confused. It seemed as though Greg had slammed her inner dignity with a sledgehammer. She felt love for Greg—at least she thought she had. She had grown to trust him. So why was he getting forcible with her?

As Greg became more aggressive, she felt an inner panic, but believed that if she just kept resisting, he would stop. At least he should stop if he respected her, shouldn't he? Finally she was crying and pleading. In the dim background she heard him laughing and telling her she would enjoy the sex.

She felt terror and disgust when he entered her. He shattered her dreams of gentleness and joy in conjugal lovemaking. "It's funny," she remembered thinking, "I'm not even here. He's doing something to my body, but I don't feel anything anymore."

When Greg finished, Kathryn lay there, eyes glazed, unmoving. He combed his hair and straightened his clothes. Then he looked at her and whispered, "Sorry if it hurt. I'll see you tomorrow."

The next morning, still in a daze, Kathryn sent Greg a letter through the campus mail explaining that she wanted to end their relationship, and that she never wished to see him again. Then she sought to put the experience out of her mind. Deep inside, however, she felt shame and fear, and a loss of faith in a loving God. After seven long years of keeping this painful secret to herself, Kathryn finally came in for counseling.

Kathryn's Inner Compass

What did Kathryn lose when she was raped? She lost her personality balance. The trauma damaged her compass of the self. For Kathryn, a new set of negative qualities took over her inner compass:

- distrust replaced love;
- fear replaced assertion;
- shame replaced weakness;
- self-doubt replaced strength.

In order to cope with this core pain, Kathryn pushed it out of her awareness and numbed herself to all feeling. All of us, to some degree, feel inner pain from the harsh blows that life sometimes gives. Our reaction to the unexpected loss of our dignity can be described as core pain.

This pain in the center of our being undermines our trust in God's love, and fragments our relationships with others. The new *Catechism* defines rape as "the forcible violation of the sexual intimacy of another person. It does injury to justice and charity. Rape deeply wounds the respect, freedom and physical and moral integrity to which every person has a right.... It is always an intrinsically evil act" (n. 2356).[7]

In past decades and even centuries rape has sometimes been gravely misunderstood. Too often rape was considered the woman's fault for provoking a man's sexual desire, or for not watching out for herself. This naive and destructive view is being rectified today. The Church is taking strong stands to minister compassion and assistance to victims of rape.

Compass counseling reawakens a person's repressed feelings, encourages the honest acceptance of one's losses, rebuilds personal identity and dignity, and restores trust in a loving God.

Releasing Core Pain

After the rape, Kathryn lost faith in God's love for her. She felt ugly inside. She assumed that God considered her undesirable and unfit for marriage because of what had happened. In our counseling sessions I helped Kathryn make a trip around the compass of the self. We got rid of the negative blocks and restored the healthy function of each point.

I started on the weakness compass point, where most people store the hurt and pain that brings them into counseling. I asked Kathryn to retell and, further, relive the rape experience. As she did, her voice captured the hurt, fear and anguish that she originally experienced. Her body tensed and shook as she allowed these long repressed emotions to surface.

Once this pain was released, an inner peace replaced her deep-seated fears. Her shame changed into a realistic acceptance of how she'd been victimized by the date rape. Her old repressed terror turned into a more normal feeling of human vulnerability. This meant that her weakness compass point was no longer stuck in shame, but was now free to register normal anxiety without escalating into panic.

Awakening Assertion

In the next session, I asked Kathryn to talk about her assertion compass point. Her face went blank. "You know, Dr. Montgomery," she said, "ever since that rape I've been easily intimidated by people. I'm afraid to stand up for myself."

Therapeutic anger is the rocket fuel that thrusts us out of another person's gravitational pull.

I invited Kathryn to do an exercise to awaken her repressed anger and begin to get it out of her system in a safe way. I placed a huge pillow in front of her and invited her to pound it with both fists, while allowing herself to feel righteous indignation about being raped. This exercise is not practice for hitting anyone. It is a safe way to release repressed rage, reminiscent of how the psalmist sometimes poured out his wrath to God in the psalms.

Kathryn started off slowly, but gathered steam with each blow. Finally, all the anger she had buried from the day of the date rape flowed out of her like molten lava. She screamed at the pillow, clawed and twisted it; then she put it on the floor and stomped on it. After this period of ventilation she looked more tranquil.

"That's what I really felt like doing when he was raping me," she exclaimed, "but I was too scared. Now I'm not afraid!" Then she added, "It feels good to be mad. He had no right to do that!"

Therapeutic anger is the rocket fuel that thrusts us out of another person's gravitational pull. Her psyche had been unconsciously orbiting the memory of Greg for years. Now she had begun to break free. As she worked through her pain, her therapy helped make her assertion pole available to serve her.

Restoring Strength

The following week I turned our attention to Kathryn's strength compass point. "How are you doing in terms of self-worth?" I asked. "Do you feel good about yourself? Is your confidence in life returning?"

"Well, I am definitely feeling stronger," she said. "But I still get twinges of guilt that I'm a second-class citizen—that I'm somehow 'used goods' because I was raped."

"You feel that God would love you more if nothing bad ever happened to you?"

"Something like that," she mumbled, looking downward.

I reached into my wallet and took out a five-dollar bill. "How much is this bill worth?" I asked.

"Five dollars," she replied.

I then crumpled the bill in my hands, dropped it on the floor and stepped on it. I gave the bill to Kathryn and asked her to unfold it again. She did so.

"How much is the bill worth now?" I asked.

She looked at it carefully and thought over her answer. "It's still worth five dollars," she said, her eyes glistening with tears. "And you're saying that I'm just as worthwhile a person as I was before the rape, right?"

"Yes," I responded. "Nothing can separate you from the

love of God. If anything, your suffering has made you all the more dear to him."

Expressing Love

Kathryn came bouncing through the door for our final session, looking like a new woman. We chatted for a while about how well she was doing. Then she brought up an issue straight out of her love compass point.

"Dr. Dan," she said, "I'm feeling so much better, but there's one thing still bothering me."

"What's that?" I asked.

"I've been thinking how confused Greg must have been to think that his sexual assault was love. He must live in some kind of hell. I hope that God helps him find himself. I really do."

I asked if she'd like to pray for Greg. As she did so, I felt my heart go out to her. Here was Kathryn, a victim of sexual abuse, praying for the one who had abused her. She was expressing her love compass point, as Jesus so often did.

Kathryn's inner healing brought a new desire for a loving relationship, and the courage to take appropriate risks toward one. She began dating again. But now she was emotionally candid with whomever she dated. She expressed her feelings and values openly and required respect. Kathryn had found personality health and the courage to love again.

Within the year she developed a trustworthy friendship with a man who was deeply attracted to her. They fell in love and married. After two years of marriage they took me out for lunch and shared with me their mutual joy. They had developed an honest, loving and Christ-centered companionship.

Any counselor can get these same results by thoroughly working around a counselee's compass of the self. The next four chapters will describe the four most common personality patterns that block many people from their true potential in Christ. These patterns stem from being stuck and exaggerating one compass point, while neglecting or avoiding the rest. These rigid patterns are one-sided ways of living that can be labeled as dependent, aggressive, withdrawn and controlling.

These labels describe the overall pattern of behavior of a counselee, without judging the person. We can speak of dependents, aggressives, withdrawers or controllers as a shorthand for describing counselees' behavior. When a person outgrows a particular pattern, the label and the pattern it represents are exchanged for greater personality wholeness in Christ.

Four
_____

Too Much Love

Counselees who love too much are always surprised to hear that an exaggerated use of love is a disservice to themselves and others. I was counseling a woman who felt terribly depressed and didn't know why.

"I do everything my husband wants," Deborah said. "I work hard keeping a clean home. We're making it financially. My son has turned out fine. Why am I so depressed?"

"Describe your husband's behavior to me," I prompted.

"Well, we've been married fifteen years, and he's pretty hard to get along with. He gets angry easily. He's always suspicious that I'm out having an affair, even if I've gone to the grocery store. When I tell him about good things that happen, he makes sour comments."

"It sounds like your husband is stuck on the assertion compass point. People stuck there have too much aggression and use anger to dominate others."

Deborah's brown eyes lit up. "That's exactly right," she exclaimed. "He's very demanding and always blows his stack."

"And what about you?" I asked. I drew a picture of the compass of the self and handed it to her. "Which compass point do you use most of the time?"

"I'm here on the love pole," she replied. "I try so hard to make people happy and keep the peace. Friends say that I've spoiled my husband."

"So you've ended up pleasing and placating him for the fifteen years of your marriage?"

"That's about it. You'd think he'd appreciate me by now. But he treats me worse than ever."

Deborah lived on a farm. I decided to use a farm-related metaphor to show the self-defeating nature of being stuck on the love compass point.

"Have you ever seen a cat catch and play with a mouse?" I asked.

"Sure, we named our cat Mouser because that's his favorite game."

"Tell me how Mouser approaches the game."

"He catches a mouse and puts it down in the center of the living room. Then he goes over to the sofa and lies down. As soon as the mouse tries to get away, Mouser leaps through the air and grabs the mouse in his teeth. He gives it a good shake and then lets it go again. He'll do this for hours. Even though the mouse gets exhausted, Mouser never loses interest in the game."

"How do you think the mouse ends up feeling?" I asked.

She paused and thought for a moment. "Trapped and depressed," she answered quietly, "just like me."

I explained, "Deborah, you may have developed early in life the dependent pattern of loving too much and used it to cope with life. But dependency is a lop-sided pattern that always fails. We need to teach you how to stand up to people and express yourself instead of living in fear of their disapproval."

Over the next several sessions, I taught Deborah how to deeply relax her mind and body, so that she would feel less anxiety in her husband's presence. Relaxation neutralizes anxiety and promotes a sense of serenity and well-being. This helps counselees concentrate on growth and change. I used a technique with Deborah called muscle melting. I had Deborah sit back in her chair and follow these instructions:

I'd like you to take three deep breaths and exhale each one slowly. That's good. Begin to allow the distractions of the day to melt away, leaving your body feeling calm and serene. You can listen to every word I say, or not pay much attention at all. Just let your body follow my instructions as you go deeper into relaxation.

Now focus your attention on your hands. Make two fists and hold them tightly while I count to three. Then release them completely. One, two, three. Notice the sensations of calm and serenity that flow into your hands as tension flows out your fingertips.

Focus on your arms, drawing your fists up to your shoulders as though lifting a heavy weight. Tighten your biceps to my count of three. One, two, three. Relax completely and breathe deeply. Enjoy the calmness and serenity in your arms.

Turning your attention to your neck, pull your shoulders upward toward your ears and hold your shoulders rigidly in place. Notice how it becomes difficult to breathe. Feel the tension in your neck and shoulders as I count to three. One, two, three. Let go completely. Your shoulders begin to melt. Tension flows out of your body. Breathing deepens. Enjoy the sensations of calmness and serenity.

Now scrunch up your facial muscles as though you were looking into the sun. Grin from ear-to-ear. Tighten your face and feel the tension. Now melt completely when I reach three. One, two, three. That's good. Calmness and serenity flow into your face and scalp.

Now focus on your mid-body and tighten your stomach as much as possible. One, two, three. Relax and breathe deeply. Every breath takes you deeper into calmness and serenity. Let your attention go to your hips and buttocks. Tighten all these muscles and notice how tension makes it difficult to breath. Feel how tension in your mid-body spreads to your upper body. One, two, three. Relax completely, letting all tension flow down your legs and out your toes. Enjoy the sensations of calmness and serenity in your mid-body.

Focusing on your legs, point your toes up toward your head and tense all your leg muscles. That's good. One, two, three. Relax completely, so your legs feel like loose rubber bands. Enjoy the calmness and serenity flowing throughout your legs.

Now turn your toes downward away from your head. Tense all your leg muscles in that direction. Hold this. One, two, three. Relax and enjoy the sensations of calmness and serenity in your legs.

Curl your toes as hard as you can. One, two, three. Now relax completely and let the sofa (or chair) do all the work of supporting you. Recall the spiritual saying that "Underneath are the everlasting arms." This is how it feels to trust in the Lord with your heart, mind and body. Enjoy the sensations of calmness and serenity that infuse your being. "Cast all your cares on him, because he cares for you" (1 Peter 4:7).

I'm going to let you remain peaceful and relaxed for one full minute in silence. Then I will count upward from one to five. At five you can open your eyes. You'll feel mentally alert and physically refreshed.

(I wait one full minute).

Okay, I'm going to count from one to five. At five, open your eyes. You'll feel mentally alert and physically refreshed. One—you begin to come up to full alertness. Two—you are able to bring the calmness and serenity back with you. Three—you feel a sensation somewhere in your body as you prepare to sit up. Four—you're aware of your physical surroundings. Five—open your eyes and enjoy feeling mentally alert and physically refreshed.

Once Deborah knew how to relax her body, I implemented imaging techniques. I asked her to imagine herself feeling calm and composed as she talked with her husband about his angry behavior.

It is often a wise move to relax your counselees, so that the anxiety within them is neutralized and they can concentrate on growth and change.

She would close her eyes and imagine a scene in which her husband was starting an argument, pouting to punish her or verbally attacking her. She would relax her body and picture herself responding more adequately. Whenever her anxiety got the best of her we would stop to discuss creative ways to respond to her husband.

In one scene she imagined him saying, "Debbie, you're ten minutes late coming back from the grocery store. I know you're having an affair. Who is it with?"

As long as she was stuck on the love compass point, Deborah would have tried to please and placate him by saying, "Oh no, honey. I promise I didn't see anyone. I love only you. Please believe me. I'd never have an affair." In fact, she had said this dozens of time to no avail.

But in this session, Deborah imagined herself being more

strong and assertive. "I'm sick of your accusations, John. I have a right to take as long as I need at the grocery store or anywhere else. I believe that you're always accusing me about having an affair to cover up your own guilt. You're always staring at other women. Instead of facing your own lust you throw up a smoke screen by saying that I'm the one who is unfaithful!"

Deborah continued taking active steps toward becoming a full-fledged person, with the rights and privileges of honest self-expression, emotional integrity and spiritual guidance from God.

This was quite a departure from her former masochistic position of accepting his abuse without question. Before long she actually had these conversations with her husband. He paid attention to what she was saying because his anger tactics no longer worked.

"I feel great!" she exclaimed a few weeks later. "I feel like I'm not a three-year-old anymore. I've always known his accusations were unfair, but I never knew how to challenge them. Now I know that what I tell my husband can make a difference."

Deborah continued taking active steps toward becoming a full-fledged person, with the rights and privileges of honest self-expression, emotional integrity and spiritual guidance from God. Gradually, the defeating patterns in her marital communication dissolved. She made remarkable progress over a year's time. Her husband slowly grew to respect her more.

The Dependent Pattern

Wrongly used, love can be a terrible trap. Counselees need to know that love never gives a license for another person to walk all over them. Masochism is a distortion of love which means that counselees think so little of themselves that others can abuse them. They have such a dire need of others' approval that they willingly surrender their dignity to get it. Masochistic love sacrifices health and well-being—supposedly to make someone else happy. Healthy love doesn't allow others to use or abuse us.

When stuck on the love compass point, counselees try to hook someone else into making them happy. They seek an all-powerful person to love and care for them. They become overly sweet and submissive to avoid conflict at all costs. The following characteristics indicate the dependent pattern:

1. Dependents place their worth in other people's hands. They want to know whether others approve of every little step they take. They care too much about whether others like them or not.

2. Their extreme outer-direction results in their being moody and petulant. If dependents enjoy constant support and encouragement, they can be cheerful. But whenever that support wavers, they become depressed.

3. Dependents are naive and gullible. They have a blind faith in authority figures. They avoid conflict with anyone. They bend over backward to keep the peace and make others happy.

4. They are fixated at the infantile level of always needing help and approval. Dependents are still connected to others by a psychological umbilical cord. It's hard for dependents to stand on their own feet and take responsibility for themselves.

5. Dependents remain bereft of an identity because they don't use their strength and assertion poles. They overly exaggerate love in the forms of pleasing, placat-

ing and complying. They fear disappointing anyone's expectations.

6. Pay them a compliment and they quickly forget it. Criticize them and they feel hurt for days.

7. Since dependents are unaware that their lack of development comes from being stuck on the love pole, they mistakenly view love as a cure-all. If only they can find a person who loves them fully, *then* everything will be all right.

8. In regard to God, dependents strive to please him by being sweet, nice and good. They prefer to believe that no one is truly evil, and that everything will work out if they just trust and obey.

9. Dependents are fortunate if they actually find a partner who has both strength *and* love. More often—because of their lack of discernment about people—they are drawn to a partner who is strong but lacks empathy, who is aggressive but lacks love.

Held Back by Self-Consciousness

Counselors, ministers and religious can secretly suffer from the dependent pattern.

A priest named Father Alberto came to me with a problem he'd never discussed before. This man had directed his parish for twelve years. I lived in the area and knew how well loved he was. Yet, as he opened his heart in counseling, Father Alberto confirmed a level of inner tension that I had sensed about him.

"Dr. Dan, you're probably going to laugh or not believe me when I say that I get so self-conscious during Mass that I often end up with a headache."

This is what I like about counseling. Counselees can say the unsayable, speak the unspeakable. They can talk openly about what's troubling them.

"Father Alberto," I said, "I believe you completely. Headaches are the body's way of voicing tension. Your body is telling you that you feel tense when you're celebrating the Mass. How long has this been going on?"

---

*By role-playing a situation,
a counselee can call up
the emotions and physical sensations
felt in the actual situation.*

"Ever since I was ordained and said my first public Mass," he said sheepishly. "About fifteen years."

"And you've never mentioned this to anyone?"

"I've been too embarrassed. I'm a priest and I'm supposed to offer Mass. It's a great privilege. Mass isn't supposed to give me a headache!"

"I see your point," I said, smiling. "But in counseling we must deal with what *is*; and the fact of the matter is that celebrating Mass causes you anxiety. When does the tension start and how do you first feel it?"

"Well," he replied, "I really enjoy walking down the aisle to the altar. I love the people and I love the Lord. But when I step up to the platform something happens. I feel tension in my neck and shoulders. Then when I'm arranging the altar for the Eucharist my hands become stiff and start trembling. Before long I have a knot in my neck and I wind up with a headache."

"Okay," I suggested, "let's act this out."

By role-playing a situation, a counselee can call up the emotions and physical sensations felt in the actual situation. Clearing off my desk, I asked Father Alberto to help push it into the center of the room. I asked him to arrange our coffee cups and saucers as though they represented the elements of the Eucharist.

"Let's pretend it's next Sunday," I said. "I want you to walk across the room to this desk. The walking represents coming down the aisle toward the altar. Stepping in front of the desk represents mounting the platform and approaching the Eucharistic table. Tell me what your body is doing and what you are thinking and feeling at each moment."

Father Alberto carried out my instructions. "I feel fine walking to the desk," he reported. But as soon as he stood directly in front of it, he blurted out, "Uh-oh. My neck just tightened up. It's starting to happen."

"Good," I said. "Counseling is the place to have a safe emergency. Nothing bad can happen here. We're going to free you from this tension. But first, what are you thinking right now?"

"I'm thinking that all the people are watching me. They expect me to go through this whole procedure perfectly. If I make a single mistake—if I'm off in my placement of anything by a fraction of an inch—they'll consider me a failure!"

"So it's like you're a defendant in a courtroom and they're the jury. One slip-up and off with your head!"

"Yes. That's exactly how I feel. My head is even starting to hurt."

"Okay, Father," I said. "I want you to think back over your life—clear back to a time in childhood when you had this same feeling."

Here I was searching for the source of his self-consciousness. I was doing a quick shuttle between the here-and-now of offering the Mass, and the there-and-then of some historical event which set in motion his dependent personality pattern. When such a connection is made, counselees have an "ah-hah" experience in which they see the past for what it was and are freed to act more creatively in the present.

Father Alberto furrowed his brow. "I used to feel this way in the presence of my mother all the time," he exclaimed. "She was very exacting. I had to do everything just right or she'd criticize me. She wasn't a mean person, just a perfectionist."

"So your neck and shoulders would feel stiff when you were around her?"

"Yes, and sometimes I'd get a headache."

"Do you see what happens when you offer Mass, Father? When you enter the church in the procession, you feel relaxed because you are with the people and you know they like you. But as soon as you get to the altar, your mother's voice takes over. Unconsciously, you see her looking over your shoulder and criticizing the slightest mistake. You project her image onto the congregation and assume that people are judging and criticizing you."

"That's exactly what I do," he said. "I believe that they're thinking thoughts like, 'Father Alberto isn't really competent. He's a nice guy, but louses up the rituals.'"

"Okay," I said, "so pretend you're back in church now and look out at the people."

He lifted his eyes and gazed at the sofa, which represented all the people in the church.

"Now imagine that your neck is a wet noodle. Let it go limp. Let your shoulders melt. Take a few deep breaths."

He let his upper torso hang more loosely. I could see his belly breathe more deeply.

"Now shut your eyes and tell me how the congregation really feels about you."

A tear flowed down his cheek. "They love me," he confided. "People are always giving me hugs and telling me what a friendly priest I am. I get lots of invitations for dinner. Even the children think I'm cool."

"And honestly, do these people expect you to be perfect?" I asked.

"No. They all know I'm not a theological giant. I'm just a simple priest with Christ's love in my heart."

"Breathe deeply and take in the truth of your own words," I urged. "Recognize that your mother's image of perfectionism is neurotic and outdated. It doesn't represent people's real experience of you. Feel free to be your real self with a simple love in your heart as you say Mass. What are you feeling right now?"

"I feel good...I feel accepted...I feel like I want to get on with the Mass." He opened his eyes. "I'm kind of excited."

"Continue with the Mass."

He went through the motions of the remainder of the Mass. I noticed a gracefulness in his body and a tenderness in his manner. He seemed to be worshipping the Lord. When he had finished, he looked up at me, eyes shining.

"What have you discovered?" I asked.

He grinned broadly. "That I'm not a little boy any more. That the people in my parish accept me as I am. That I don't have to pay attention to Mom's critical voice in my head. That the Lord wants me to relax and enjoy his presence during the Mass."

"Very good. Remember this feeling of freedom. Are you aware of anything else?"

"Yes, but I'm not sure I can say it. It feels like when I'm my real self at the altar and don't need to impress anybody, I enjoy what I'm doing. I never realized how much my self-consciousness was holding me back."

"That's plenty of insight for one session," I concluded. "I'd like you to lead us in prayer and then apply what you've learned to the Mass next Sunday. We can talk over what happens during our next session."

We bowed our heads. "Father," he prayed softly, "thank you that I feel more relaxed in your presence. Help me enjoy leading your people in worship next Sunday. Bless Dr. Dan. In the name of the Father, Son and Holy Spirit. Amen."

When we met the following week, Father Alberto reported that our experiment had worked. His body remembered how to relax. His mind caught the critical voice of his mother and told her to be quiet. His heart brimmed with love for God and for his congregation. His old self-consciousness quieted, Father Alberto's spirit soared.

Tips for Counseling Dependents

Dependent counselees transfer their indiscriminate need for everyone's approval right into the counseling setting. As a counselor, you've got to resist being trapped by dependents' sweetness, niceness, politeness and attempts to be very good counselees.

If their trap works, you'll feel afraid to confront them with the truth of their rigid pattern—the fact that they are filled with anxiety, lack an adequate identity, camouflage their resentment of others, turn negative emotions into physical complaints, and run away from opportunities for greater autonomy.

Dependent persons are used to superficial living. They don't want to see any evil in the world or in themselves. You need courage as a counselor to upset their Pollyanna world view. If you don't, they'll stay stuck exactly where they are, pleasing and placating others while remaining secretly depressed and resentful.

How do we as counselors confront dependents without devastating them? We break the news gently by exploring how they first acquired dependent trends in childhood and adolescence. We ask, "Who gave you the notion to be terribly concerned with what everyone thinks about you?" We help them discover when they learned to get people's attention through good behavior, but experienced people's disapproval for expressing their real feelings. We probe why, instead of standing up for themselves, they let other people take advantage of them.

We help dependents connect their years of secret suffering with the realization that they are afraid to assert themselves, can't say no without feeling guilty and don't know what they want out of life.

As a counselor, you've got to resist being trapped by dependents' sweetness, niceness, politeness and attempts to be very good counselees.

Offer your dependent counselees abundant praise whenever they express real needs or opinions, or whenever they show any form of inner direction versus outer-directedness. Inner direction is essential to personality health. Christ showed inner direction when he followed his internal marching orders from the Holy Spirit. Dependents must learn this same lesson.

Just as Jesus made choices in lifestyle, self-expression and spiritual vocation that did not depend on other people's demands or expectations, dependent counselees must learn to trust their own hunches, hearts' desires and inner truth in Christ.

Another trap dependents will set for you is to ask question after question instead of actively taking growth steps. They try to get you to take responsibility for what they do next. The temptation is to feel flattered as a counselor when they tell you how wise and wonderful you are, and how they can't get along without you. However, if you get hooked by this ploy, they remain as dependent as ever.

You must skillfully frustrate their needs to lean on you. Ask them how they feel and wait for them to spell it out. Ask them what they want from life. Put them on the spot when they say that their needs are not really important. Ask them if they want to grow into adulthood or if they are content to remain childlike, innocent—and miserable!

Whenever dependents take real growth stretches into the strength and assertion compass points, they feel guilty at first, because the last thing they want to do is make waves or step on someone's toes. Point out that this is a false guilt based on having an overly strict conscience.

Dependents are usually overly socialized to begin with. That's why they believe that just being nice will get them through life. But Jesus wasn't nice all the time. Sometimes he got frustrated, angry and confrontive. And if dependent counselees want to become Christlike, they've got to share Christ's courage to be non-conformist when fairness and justice are at stake.

Become the accepting parent that your dependent counselees never had. Accept them when they finally open up about their anger toward others, their secret depression, their fears of God and their disgust with their own niceness. Now they're being honest, and your acceptance of their negative feelings and thoughts helps them to become more so.

Most of all, redefine their sense of social responsibility. Most dependents believe they are in the world exclusively to make other people happy. Challenge this with the idea that they are in the world to become fully developed personalities— capable of assertion as well as love, and of strength as well as weakness. They need to learn how to hold their own in creative conflict with others, how to stand up for who they really are.

They also need to become more real and emotionally expressive with God. Have them pray in front of you. Encourage them to be less mousy, less sweet in their language, less placating toward God. Model a more balanced form of praying in which whatever comes out—positive and negative—is expressed to God. Help them discover that God rejoices in their honesty.

Counseling Growth Stretches

1. Dependents are afraid to express their personal tastes, desires and preferences. You can say to your counselee, "This week tell one other person about your favorite color, food, music, hobby and book. Express yourself straight out. This makes you more visible in the world and allows people around you to understand what's inside—what makes you unique."

2. Challenge their fear of making waves. You can encourage them, "Clearly state your own bias or opinions or beliefs in conversations with at least three people this week. For instance, if someone is a Republican and you are a Democrat, say so. If someone loved a movie and you hated it, say so. You must learn that you have the right to disagree without being a bad person. You must practice expressing your opinions so that others can respect your point of view."

3. Tell your counselee to carefully observe the behavior of people they know who can diplomatically express themselves without hiding, compromising or being belligerent. They can internalize such models by acting the same way— copying another's healthy assertion until assertion flows spontaneously from their own personality. They can give themselves a test by tactfully negotiating for something they really want or need in a calm but firm manner.

4. Ask them to handle someone's rejection or disapproval by telling themselves that they are not in the world to live up to others' expectations. They are to be patriotic to themselves and refuse to feel guilty. If someone points out a fault, they can bring to mind a good point about themselves. Encourage them

to ask Christ to strengthen their self-identity so that they can stand up for themselves without apology.

5. Suggest they ponder the following Scriptures, asking the Holy Spirit to apply these verses to their lives. Suggest they write in a journal what these verses mean to their personality growth.

> *2 Timothy 1:7:* God did not give us a spirit of cowardice, but rather a spirit of power and of love and of self-discipline.

> *Romans 8:31:* If God is for us, who is against us?

> *Proverbs 4:5, 6:* Get wisdom; get insight.... Do not forsake her, and she will keep you; love her, and she will guard you.

> *Matthew 10:16:* Be wise as serpents and innocent as doves.

> *Galatians 1:10:* Am I now seeking human approval, or God's approval? Or am I trying to please people? Or am I trying to please men? If I were still pleasing people, I would not be a servant of Christ.

> *Romans 12:2:* Do not be conformed to this world, but be transformed by the renewing of your minds.

> *John 14:27:* Peace I leave with you; my peace I give to you. I do not give to you as the world gives. Do not let your hearts be troubled, and do not let them be afraid.

6. Encourage them to make an independent decision and follow through on it no matter what. It may mean signing up for a community college class, buying something nice for themselves, joining a health spa, resigning from a committee, or joining a Twelve-Step group (Co-Dependents Anonymous, or "CODA" is a good one for dependent types). Help them resist the temptation to ask people's opinion about their decision. The point is to take responsibility for their lives and make autonomous choices because it seems right to them.

The Positives of the Love Compass Point

When the love compass point is intact, with the corresponding rhythms of assertion and strength, counselees experience emotions of caring, affection and joy. Pleasing and placating are cleared away so that counselees can take the emotional and spiritual risks that compass living requires. Counselees feel like they have a creative voice in how things go. They take responsibility for thinking, feeling and acting.

Existential psychologist Rollo May writes about the need for integrating love and will:

> We *will* the world, create it by our decision, our fiat, our choice; and we *love* it, give it affect, energy, power to love and change us as we mold and change it. This is what it means to be fully related to one's world.[8]

Love that is balanced is more than a feeling; it is a commitment to the highest good of ourselves and other people. Healthy love involves willing God's loving intentions for his creation, in our little corner of the world. The development of healthy love brings with it a tenderness toward existence.

Jesus said: "By this everyone will know that you are my disciples, if you have love for one another" (John 13:35). This is how God relates to humanity and how he inspires us to relate to each other. Love is the lifeblood of the balanced personality.

Five

Too Much Anger

Norman was a major in the Marine Corps who came to see me on a dare. An imposing man with a neck like a bulldog, Norm's laserbeam eyes could pierce right through you.

I'd counseled a friend of his named Bobby. Norm had noticed that Bobby was undergoing a considerable change in his aggressive attitude. At first Norman chided Bobby for showing a new humility and compassion for others. "Bobby, you're becoming a big softy," he razzed him one evening over a beer. "You used to be tough as nails. What's wrong with you?"

"Promise not to laugh?" asked Bobby.

"Sure," said Norman.

"I've been going to counseling for a couple of months."

Norm broke out laughing.

Bobby continued, "You know the problems I was having with my wife. I went into counseling to set her straight. But I found out that I'm the biggest problem. Dr. Montgomery said that I'm a superior top dog who needs to control everyone. He said I'm the one who's destroying our marriage by dogging Betty all the time."

"So what are you supposed to do—roll over and play dead?" Norm sneered.

"No," Bobby replied. "I just need to quit feeling superior all the time. I need to quit trying to win every argument and start listening to her. It's not easy, but I'm learning to admit my weaknesses and show her love."

"Only wimps do that," protested Norm.

Bobby smiled. "No, I'm finally doing something worthwhile. I dare you to make an appointment with Dr. Dan."

————————◆————————

Aggressive counselees use two major tactics
when they come into counseling.
Either they pour on the charm
to convince you how perfect they are,
or they draw you into a fight and walk out.

————————◆————————

Norman stiffened his neck. "That'll be a cold day in hell," he retorted. "No, I take that back. I'll make an appointment just to give that S.O.B. a piece of my mind!"

That's how Norman came in for counseling, according to what he and Bobby later told me. In taking that step, Norm took a giant stride toward growing beyond his aggressive tendencies.

During our first session, Norm defended his highly paranoid philosophy of life. He made statements like: "I keep people on a short leash because they can't be trusted." "I use anger to keep people in line." "Only fools believe in love."

I resisted the impulse to argue with Norm and instead listened intently. This was particularly difficult because he slipped several zingers into our conversation. "You shrinks don't know a thing about the real world." "Psychologists like you live off people's misery—you take their money and keep them dependent on you."

Aggressive counselees use two major tactics when they come into counseling. Either they pour on the charm to convince you they don't need help, or they draw you into a fight and walk out. I kept praying for the Lord to help me see Norman as Christ saw him—a scared man trying to find meaning by feeling superior. I felt a degree of empathy for the loneliness and emptiness that I knew haunted Norm.

Being diplomatic but firm, I said, "Norm, I don't need your money. I don't want to counsel you unless you want me to. If you want to go it alone and feel superior to the world, I wish you all the best. But I'm wondering if you ever feel lonely inside your castle of solitude?"

Apparently, this was the last thing he expected to hear, because a thin veil of tears flashed across his eyes. He cleared his throat. "Everybody gets lonely. We're all in this life alone."

"Do you ever wish you could experience love?" I asked. "Something enduring? Something special? Something real?"

"Sure I've thought about it," he said. "I just don't think it's real. I think everybody is out for themselves. If you can show me differently I'll be impressed."

I drew the following compass on a sheet of paper. I purposefully exaggerated the assertion compass point, while shrinking the other points.

"Norm," I said, "here is a picture of your personality. Everyone has these four compass points. You've been exaggerating the assertive compass point throughout your adult life."

"What does that mean?" he asked, holding the paper in his hands.

"My guess is that either as a kid or in your career as a Marine, you learned to get your way by overpowering others

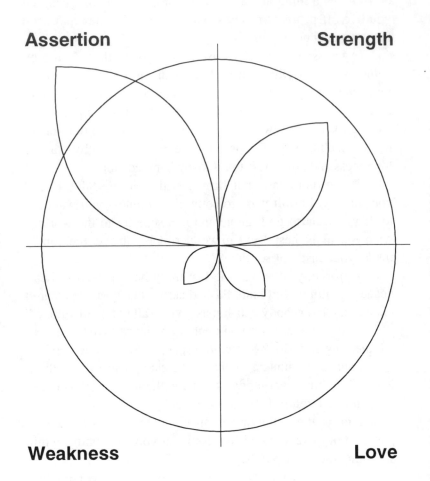

Assertion

Strength

Weakness

Love

with aggression. You didn't pay attention to people's feelings as long as you got your way. Does that sound accurate?"

Norm's eyes narrowed. "My ex-wife says I'm stubborn and proud of it. I always figured I couldn't help it."

Over the next few months of counseling,
I kept hammering home the
self-defeating nature of his aggressiveness.

"No," I assured him, "blaming and attacking others is a personal choice. There's a lot of goodness in you that wants to come out. But if you stay out of balance you'll be helpless to ever change."

He winced at my words. The veil of tears reappeared in his eyes. I interpreted this as an inner longing to be a more balanced person. "I'll have to think about this," he said. "I'll call you if I want another appointment. Can I take this with me?" he asked, waving the paper.

"Sure. Give me a call if you want to continue. I believe you can become a commander with compassion for his troops. You can inspire them by building them up, not tearing them down."

We shook hands and Norm left. Two days later his secretary called and made a second appointment for him. Over the next few months of counseling, I kept hammering home the self-defeating nature of Norm's aggressiveness. We went over the times in high school and adult life when his anger backfired, leaving him all alone. We looked at how anger interfered with his education, career and marriage. He began to take growth stretches to expand his personality.

On the weakness point, he practiced admitting when he was wrong, handling anxiety without getting angry, and developing patience with himself and others. For the first time in his life, he asked God for help.

On the love point, he worked on complimenting others, listening to people's feelings, and caring about his soldiers instead of badgering them.

On the strength point, Norm tried cooperating with his peers instead of competing with them, contributing his ideas without dominating, and esteeming others instead of blaming them.

Norm's therapy lasted a year. During that time he made amends to his ex-wife and developed a friendship with her. He related to other officers and the enlisted men with greater diplomacy. Near the end of the year Norm's unit threw a party for him. At the party, a fellow officer commented that Norm was no longer a petty tyrant.

The hardest part of working with aggressives is creating, with God's help, the motivation for change. They fear giving up what has worked in the past—blaming and attacking those around them. But once they see how self-defeating this life style is, they can find the love and friendship that has always eluded them.

The Aggressive Pattern

Counselees stuck on the assertion compass point cope with inner pain by blaming, attacking and venting on those around them. The following symptoms indicate a person who is aggressively out of balance.

1. Aggressives view life as a dog-eat-dog world. If they don't get their way, they make plans to get even. They hold grudges for years and trust no one but themselves. The main emotions they feel are bitterness, spite and hatred.

2. They abuse others without feeling guilty. They view spouses and children as their private possessions and become furious if not strictly obeyed.

3. They are insanely jealous of their spouses. They demand to know where their spouses are at all times. They closely watch and control their kids. They dish out punishment to keep family members in line.

4. They are stubborn and proud of it. Their views are always right. They have nothing to learn and are suspicious of anyone who might teach them something. They consider others' views as irrelevant to their decisions and actions.

5. They intimidate others with icy glares, raised eyebrows, pointed fingers, cold shoulders and long lectures. They may threaten abandonment or physical violence if they don't get their way. They are masters at controlling people through anger. They take offense over the slightest issue.

6. They can be quite charming if this gets them what they want, but underneath this facade they remain tough-minded realists. They live life on *their* terms.

7. If someone threatens them, they get stronger. If someone criticizes them, they get meaner. If someone humiliates them, they get even.

8. They conceal their shortcomings and problems because they feel it is nobody else's business. They believe that what others know will be used against themselves. They don't let anybody get too close.

9. They are unwilling to "give in," even on trivial issues, because compromise is a sign of weakness, which they scorn.

10. If they are religious, they believe that God is an angry God. They believe that God disdains those who are weak or sentimental and that he hates people who are different from themselves. They serve God by threatening people so that they will obey.

Tips for Counseling Aggressives

One secret in successfully counseling aggressive people is to realize that they don't really want to be counseled. They usually come into therapy because they are in trouble with a spouse, they keep losing jobs, or they've run aground with the law. Give up your need to help them unless they personally choose to work with you.

The wisest thing you can do
is relax your body, breathe deeply,
trust in the healing presence
of the Holy Spirit and relate to them
with the balance of
your own personality compass.

How do you tell if you've got an aggressive counselee on your hands? Easy. They take issue with you right away. They try to pull you into a power struggle so they can intimidate you. Or—if they can get away with it—they'll charm you into adopting their point of view.

To counsel aggressives, you've got to stay calm when they blame and attack you. How do you keep your cool under fire? The best strategy is to relax your body, keep breathing deeply, and trust in the healing presence of the Holy Spirit. Relate to them with the balance of your own personality compass. Don't take the bait when they try to argue with you. Feed back to them the ploys they use to evade personal growth. Trust the counseling process.

Don't be afraid to be assertive. Just make sure you also reflect their feelings and points of view so that they feel understood and not just confronted.

Aggressives are masters at creating body tension in counselors, making us walk on eggshells. You may need a long hot bath, a workout at the gym or a good jog to get rid of the tension you incur during a session.

Counseling Growth Stretches

1. Tell aggressive counselees that they need to smash the illusion that their anger is advantageous. Give them the following homework:

Stop yourself five times this week when you start to get angry. Keep your mouth shut and tell yourself that you are becoming a sensitive person who can hear and handle people's opinions, feelings and behavior.

Take several deep breaths to help calm yourself when you start to get angry. Pray for God to help you develop tolerance and forgiveness. Practice helping others instead of berating them.

2. Suggest that they make amends to two people whom they've abused with their anger. They are to ask for forgiveness and not explode, regardless of the outcome.

3. Encourage aggressive counselees to talk to friends about their anxieties and weaknesses. Point out that by becoming more transparent they can experience other people's love for them.

4. Give them the following Scriptures to ponder. Invite them to pray for the Holy Spirit's comfort, guidance and wisdom.

Galatians 5:19-20: Now the works of the flesh are obvious...enmities, strife, jealousy, anger, quarrels, dissensions, factions, envy....

James 1:20: For your anger does not produce God's righteousness.

Proverbs 19:19: A violent-tempered person will pay the penalty; if you effect a rescue, you will only have to do it again.

Proverbs 15:1: A soft answer turns away wrath, but a harsh word stirs up anger.

Ephesians 6:4: Fathers, do not provoke your children to anger, but bring them up in the discipline and instruction of the Lord.

2 Timothy 3:1-5: You must understand this, that in the last days distressing times will come. For people will be lovers of themselves, lovers of money, boasters, arrogant, abusive, disobedient to their parents, ungrateful, unholy, inhuman, implacable, slanderers, profligates, brutes, haters of good, treacherous, reckless, swollen with conceit, lovers of pleasure rather than lovers of God, holding to the outward form of godliness but denying its power. Avoid them!

Romans 12:18: So far as it depends on you, live peaceably with all.

5. Suggest that they become more generous. They can serve others rather than getting their way, give gifts without expecting repayment, and remember birthdays or graduations with a card.

Positives of the Assertion Compass Point

The test of maturity on the assertion pole is whether counselees can assert themselves without being wrathful or vengeful. Personality balance means that they can take stands without burning bridges and express feelings while respecting others. In healthy assertion they may feel angry or resentful, but they learn to utilize diplomatic communication instead of blowing people away.

Diplomatic assertion serves the ends of love and justice in the world. It empowers counselees to fight against unfairness and exploitation—to speak the truth in love.

Growth in the assertion compass point means saying, "I am expressive," "I can challenge," "I can confront" and "I can make a difference." Just as compassion flows from the love compass point, the virtue of courage arises from a healthy use of the assertion pole.

By employing compass counseling growth strategies, formerly aggressive counselees can end up with personalities balanced by courage and caring.

Six

Too Much Weakness

A young woman with red hair and green eyes came to see me in a church counseling center. Pamela looked shy and withdrawn when I first met her. She kept her eyes glued to the floor. Her voice was hesitant. She kneaded her fingers together every now and then.

Pamela attended a nearby college. Her present problem was fear of leaving her dorm room. She would get out for classes and cafeteria meals, but other than that she lived like a hermit in a cave.

"My room is my sanctuary," she told me. "I feel safe there. All I do is study, so I earn high grades. But I'm worried because I don't have any friends. I'm too shy to attend dances, sports events or even talk to my professors. Will I always be like this?"

Pam had a valid question. People can stay stuck in rigid personality patterns for decades or even a lifetime.

"I'm glad you've come to talk about this," I said. To answer her question, I showed her the compass of the self. She looked on with great interest as I briefly described what it's like to be stuck on each compass point. When I spoke about the weakness pole, she said, "That's me—I'm stuck there. I'm afraid of people and I never try anything new. I just sit on the sidelines and watch life go by."

I asked Pamela to write me a letter before our next session, telling me the highlights of her life story. I knew that if she was like other withdrawn counselees, writing about her past would feel less threatening than talking about it.

Two days later, she sent the following letter in the campus mail:

> I was very close to my daddy until the third grade. He always hugged me when he came home from work, and let me sit on his lap. My favorite thing to do with him was to make popcorn in the kitchen.
>
> Suddenly, when I was in the third grade, Daddy turned on me. When I tried to sit on his lap, he'd push me off. When I tried to talk to him, he'd tell me to shut up. One day he got really mad and left bruises on my arms.
>
> When I was a teenager, a family therapist told me that Daddy had turned from a social drinker into a full-blown alcoholic when I was nine. He got hostile with everyone. My mother was afraid and ashamed. She kept his drinking a secret from me.
>
> I tried a few more times to get Daddy's attention so that he would be proud of me instead of being angry. But soon I learned that any attention from him was negative and painful. I decided to withdraw and give up my need for his love. At least I'd feel safe this way.
>
> When Daddy got killed in a car accident last year, I felt furious that he'd abandoned me forever! Now, I ache for his love, but I hear only his critical words ringing in my head.

In our next session, I helped Pamela to understand that her early experiences with her father predisposed her to believe that everyone else would be critical of her, too. I explained that at college she was projecting her father's negative image onto her professors and peers, and therefore feeling afraid of them. She unconsciously assumed that people were out to ridicule and reject her.

For our third session, I asked Pamela to bring in a family scrapbook. I wanted to view the body language of her father, mother and herself. A picture is worth a thousand words. She brought in a family video that had been converted from old home movies.

There was a friendly scene of Pam playing catch with her dad when she was about six. But at her tenth birthday party, the video showed him yelling at her for not looking directly into the bright lights of the camera. He told her she was ruining the party by not letting him take good pictures. She collapsed into tears and ran out of the room.

We connected these historical experiences with her current fears that people didn't like her. She began to understand how she had become stuck on the weakness compass point and why she hid in her room. We were making her unconscious more conscious.

"I think your dad's constant criticisms made you feel like you were always falling short," I said. "I imagine you became afraid to try new things, knowing that nothing you did was ever good enough for him. Is that right?"

Pam's eyes widened. "That rings a bell," she exclaimed. "I remember in junior high I tried one last time to make him say something good about me. He was always working with tools downstairs. I spent a whole Saturday building a little bookcase for him. I tied a red bow around it. On Sunday morning, I took him downstairs and showed him the bookcase. He got furious and said I was stupid for wasting the wood. I broke into tears and ran to my room."

I said, "So no matter how hard you tried to get some positive attention, it was never enough. I think this is why you gave up on people and decided to live like a hermit in a cave."

She nodded. "That's what I'm doing even though he's dead now."

"We need to help you stretch into your strength and assertion compass points. Then you'll be bolder about expressing yourself and getting to know people."

"How can I start?" she asked.

"We'll take that step in the next session," I responded.

I began the fourth session by placing two chairs opposite each other.

"Let's begin with an imaginary encounter with your father," I suggested. "I know that he's gone now. But you need to talk to him just the same. You need to take responsibility for your own self-worth."

"How can I talk to him when he's dead?"

"Just sit in this chair and picture your father sitting in the other chair. Tell him what you've been holding inside you."

She sat down, faced the other empty chair and swallowed hard.

"Picture the last time you tried to talk to him," I coached. "What was stuck in your craw that you want to tell him now?"

Tears formed in her eyes. "Daddy, you used to be so fun when I was a little girl. Then you started drinking and everything changed. You got mean and bossy. According to you, I couldn't do anything right. But now you're gone and I have a life to live." She paused.

"Tell him how you're going to live your life," I suggested.

"Daddy, your life turned out awful and I'm not going to make the same mistake. I'm going to believe in myself from now on. I don't need your approval for what I do!"

"Say that last line again, louder," I said.

"I DON'T NEED YOUR APPROVAL ANYMORE! I'M APPROVING OF MYSELF!"

"Tell your father what you're approving of in yourself," I urged.

"I like that I'm not afraid to work. I study hard and I know I'll be reliable when I get a job. I like that I'm a lot more patient than you were. I like that I don't drink or do drugs. I like that I have a relationship with God."

"That's good," I said. "Now relax and take a big breath. You are standing up to your father, and you're doing a very good job. How do you feel right now?"

The edges of her mouth turned upward in the trace of a smile. "I feel good. I think I've needed to say these things for years. I was always too afraid, but I don't feel scared right now."

"What do you feel?" I asked.

"Peaceful. Kind of excited."

"Talk to your father one more minute. What else do you need to say?"

"Daddy," she said, her voice softer now. "I know you had a hard life, but you brought a lot of it on yourself. Now that you're gone I don't hold it against you. I love you, but I'm not going to pay attention to your criticisms anymore. I'm a good person with a lot going for me. I have a right to be happy." She looked up at me. "There," she declared, "I'm finished."

I gave her a Kleenex to dab her eyes. Serenity shone on her face.

"What you've done is very courageous," I said. "You've just felt the power of your assertion, strength and love compass points. You need all of these parts of your personality in order to be alive and expressive. I want to encourage you to keep incorporating them into your personality."

"I understand a lot better how my compass works," she said. "It feels good to take responsibility."

I closed our counseling session with a healing prayer. "Lord, thank you for helping Pam get out of her weakness today. Now let the Holy Spirit stream through her and flood her with your love and power. In Jesus' name. Amen."

When we met for our final session, I could sense Pam's new confidence. Her face looked fresh and her voice was animated. In balancing assertion and strength with her love and weakness, Pam was becoming more whole. In her senior year, Pam gave the valedictorian address for the graduating class. Her new friends cheered her on.

The Withdrawn Pattern

When stuck on the weakness compass point, counselees are convinced of their own helplessness. They give up and give in, adjusting to situations that most people would find intolerable. They escape their pain through sleeping, procrastinating, fantasizing or walking around in a perpetual daze.

The following behaviors and emotions can usually be observed in a first session. They betray the withdrawn pattern of personality:

1. They long to be liked, but are convinced that they are unlikeable. They watch for the slightest sign of rejection from people. Their most common feeling is sadness. They often report that the body feels numb. The numbness comes from detaching themselves from vital feelings and sensations in an attempt to reduce anxiety.

2. They are shy and hypersensitive. They fantasize that people feel negatively toward them. They are prone to feelings of inferiority, panic attacks, shame, sadness and self-pity.

3. They are so preoccupied with fears and insecurities that they constantly imagine themselves in danger. They always pursue the course of greatest safety, which is to take no risks whatever. They draw an *imaginary circle* around themselves which no one can penetrate.

4. They are a basket case of "nerves" around people. They often experience palpitations, sweating, blushing or stomach cramps. In social situations they "shut down" by standing in the corner or leaving at the first opportunity. If they are called upon to speak, their minds can go blank. They avoid direct eye contact. Only by *active withdrawal* can they protect themselves. Only in being alone do they gain a sense of relief.

5. Their goals are negative: not to be involved; not to need anyone; not to allow others to influence them.

6. They discount compliments by believing that people are putting them on. They see others as setting them up for ridicule. They think, "If you really knew me, you wouldn't say that."

7. Their desires for affection are repressed and constrained. Life is a party they can never attend.

8. Their relationship with God is equally uncomfortable. Even though they may believe in him, they are convinced that he doesn't like them. They feel that God would accept the whole world before he would choose them as friends, that he despises them because of their weaknesses, and that he knows what cowards and failures they are.

Special Counseling Tips

You can spot someone who is stuck in the weakness pattern almost immediately. The hand shake is limp. They avoid eye contact and hesitate when speaking. It's as if the person doesn't have enough energy to communicate with you, and may lack the verbal skills to articulate what's really wrong.

We need to keep in mind that people stuck in weakness have been wounded by life: a harsh or rejecting parent; a brutal older brother or sister; a traumatic experience of abuse in middle school or high school. There will be something in their life history that accounts for the turtle-like existence they now lead.

The bottom line is that the withdrawn person expects and may even try to elicit frustration or rejection from the counselor. When we observe the withdrawn pattern, we adopt a counseling strategy based on patience and long-suffering. We purposefully set low expectations for these counselees, so that they can take small, easy steps toward gradual progress. Even so, we must keep spurring them on or else they will sabotage counseling by doing nothing.

How do we get them growing without overwhelming them? How do we encourage them to take responsibility for themselves without making them feel guilty? How do we help them get rid of their procrastination, excuses and self-pity?

Counselors handle withdrawn people in much the same way that Special Olympics coaches train physically challenged individuals. We give lots of love, encouragement and grace. We listen patiently to their fears and insecurities. Yet we refuse to take "I can't" for an answer. We cheer them forward with every tiny step of progress they make.

When I suggested to one withdrawn counselee that he join a guitar club to make some friends (playing the guitar was his only hobby), he protested, "So you want me to jump into the deep end and start swimming?"

Building on his analogy, I said, "No, I'm encouraging you to wade in from ankle-deep water to knee-deep water. When you're comfortable there, we'll take a few steps into shoulder high water where you can practice swimming. When you've mastered that, you can plunge into deeper water until you're comfortable there, too."

We must bear in mind that withdrawn counselees are detached for a reason. By probing about their childhood and teenage years, it will soon become apparent what happened to place such great anxiety within them. We show empathy for their pain, but point out that childhood is now over. They have a second chance as adults to learn how to live and communicate with others.

———————————

When we observe the withdrawn pattern,
we adopt a counseling strategy
based on patience and long-suffering.
We purposefully set low expectations for
these counselees, so that they can take small,
easy steps toward gradual progress.

———————————

We work to develop and strengthen their practical communication skills. We role-play how to initiate and terminate conversations. We discuss how to meet people and maintain friendships. We help them identify and express a wide range of human feelings. By becoming positive parent surrogates who really believe in them, we stand in the gap of the poor parenting they may have received.

By paying attention to their interests and talents, we impart to them the will to live and develop themselves. We pray inwardly that they'll develop the moxie to handle whatever life challenges lie ahead. While it is slow and painstaking work to counsel withdrawn people, it gives immense rewards when we see them blossom.

Counseling Growth Stretches

1. Suggest to your counselees that they make a conscious decision to outgrow the withdrawn pattern. Encourage them to pray for the Holy Spirit's daily assistance in rooting out nega-

tive self-talk. Instead of thinking, "I'm stupid," they can think, "I'm as intelligent as the next person." Instead of thinking, "I'm unattractive," they can think, "I have my own unique looks and can improve them if I wish." Instead of thinking, "I am unlikeable," they can think, "people will like me just as I am."

Share your belief that God doesn't think they are weak and hopeless—that God specializes in loving the people who need him the most.

2. Do a joint inventory of their gifts and talents. Assist them in actively developing their skills, talents and potentials. Suggest they use community college, church or company resources to develop their strengths.

If they're athletic, suggest getting a coach to work with them. If they're artistic they can hire a tutor. If they need help with finances, child care or housing, they can seek out a community agency. Honor whatever cries out for expression within them. Gradually, they can get off the sidelines and into the mainstream of life.

3. If need be, they can join a Twelve-Step group to receive help and fellowship in their area of need. For instance, if they have an eating disorder, they can join Overeaters Anonymous. If they were abused as a child, they can join a Children of Adult Alcoholics or Incest Survivors group.

4. Give counselees a list of the following Scriptures for meditation during counseling. Ask them to write a brief response about how each verse invites them to the adventure of living. Encourage them to call upon God to bring them comfort and personality balance through these verses:

> *Isaiah 40:28, 31:* The Lord is the everlasting God, the Creator of the ends of the earth.... Those who wait for the Lord shall renew their strength, they shall mount up with wings like eagles, they shall run and not be weary, they shall walk and not faint.

John 14:27: Peace I leave with you; my peace I give to you. I do not give to you as the world gives. Do not let your hearts be troubled, and do not let them be afraid.

Psalm 27:1: The Lord is my light and my salvation; whom shall I fear? The Lord is the stronghold of my life; of whom shall I be afraid?

Romans 8:38-39: For I am convinced, that neither death, nor life, nor angels, nor rulers, nor things present, nor things to come, nor height, nor depth, nor anything else in all creation, will be able to separate us from the love of God in Christ Jesus our Lord.

Philippians 4:19: And my God will fully satisfy every need of yours according to his riches in glory in Christ Jesus.

2 Timothy 1:7: For God did not give us a spirit of cowardice, but rather a spirit of power and of love and of self-discipline.

1 John 4:18: There is no fear in love, but perfect love casts out fear.

Romans 8:28: We know that all things work together for good for those who love God, who are called according to his purpose.

Jude 24-25: Now to him who is able to keep you from falling, and to make you stand without blemish in the presence of his glory with rejoicing, to the only God our Savior, be glory, majesty, power, and authority, before all time now and forever. Amen.

5. Suggest that taking a few risks is better than sitting out the game of life on the bench. Praise them for the tiniest successes.

Suggest a homework assignment of walking up to a group of people and joining them. As they persist in socially empowering exercises, their former irrational fears will vanish. They'll eventually find a tangible peace in acting naturally around others.

Positives of the Weakness Compass Point

All human beings feel weak and inadequate from time to time. Some cover it up more than others. But weakness is no sin. In our weakness we are made strong, because we look beyond ourselves. In healthy weakness, we learn to admit our limitations and freely ask the Holy Spirit to comfort us.

---

*Life can become bleak for a season,
but if we confess our needs
to God and friends, then stunning setbacks
are often transformed into
victories of growth and recovery.*

A healthy acceptance of weakness means sometimes saying, "I am imperfect," "I feel vulnerable," "I need help," and "There is growth in the valley."

The weakness pole offers us much to learn. This compass point must be the Lord's favorite, because it leads to humility on our part, and a blessed ability to empathize with those who are in pain.

As counselors, we help counselees accept occasional weakness without magnifying it and feeling like failures. I explain to my counselees that seasons of weakness are times for soul-searching, royal reminders that we need to rely upon God throughout life. The weakness compass point reminds us that apart from Christ, we can do nothing.

Weakness forms the spiritual tension of personality, the fact that we can affirm meaning even in the midst of evil, pain and mortality. Life can become bleak for a season, but if we confess our needs to God and friends, then stunning setbacks are often transformed into victories of growth and recovery.

Reinhold Niebuhr shows us the creative rhythm between strength and weakness in a balanced personality: "God, grant me the serenity to accept the things I cannot change, the courage to change the things I can, and the wisdom to know the difference."

Seven

Too Much Strength

C ora, a tall woman with wire-rimmed glasses and short black hair, headed the religious education program in a large parish. The priest had asked me to do some small group work with Cora's staff. He had sensed a lot of tension among them and hoped we could create a more harmonious environment.

When I first met her, I was struck by Cora's firm handshake and serious demeanor. She called me into her office minutes before our first group session. "Dr. Montgomery," she said, "I hope you can lecture the teachers on how they should be more obedient to authority. There's too much individuality here. Things would run more smoothly if everyone did what I said."

I recognized the controlling personality pattern at work in Cora's life. Her strength lacked humility and love.

During the first group session I spoke about the compass of the self. I explained that when our personalities are out of balance, we create an atmosphere of tension in those around us. Many teachers nodded in agreement. A few glanced directly at

Cora. I discussed the self-defeating nature of dependent, aggressive, withdrawn and controlling personality patterns. I showed how these patterns distort relationships and rob people of their full potential. To warm up the group for self-disclosure, I shared some of my own personality foibles.

In adulthood, we have a second chance to revise our personality assumptions and relate to others with wiser principles.

After our break, I invited people to disclose what they had learned about themselves. To my surprise, Cora's hand went up first.

"I feel embarrassed to admit this," she confided to the group, "but I expected Dr. Montgomery to tell all of you that you should follow my rules and regulations. But when he talked about the compass of the self, I discovered that I'm a major league controller!"

I walked over to Cora and shook her hand. "Cora, you just took your first growth stretch toward becoming a more balanced person. By admitting a weakness, you've expressed humility. This is the opposite of being stuck on the strength compass point. You just modeled what it's like to take a risk and become more real."

I turned to the group. "Is there anyone else who'd like to own up to an insight into your personality?"

Over the next hour, seven women and two men took leaps of faith and talked openly about the patterns they recognized in themselves. I complimented them all, pointing out that admitting our needs for growth is what the kingdom of God is all about. In a circle of prayer, we ended the session by saying the Our Father together. The teachers gave hugs of reconciliation on the way out.

During the next four sessions the group made progress in developing an open style of communication and more democratic methods for handling the issues they faced. After the group work was completed, Cora asked to see me for an individual session.

"Dr. Montgomery," she said, "my husband calls me a control freak. I never understood what he meant before. But now I get it. He's saying that I'm too hard on him and our three girls. I'm always correcting everyone. I learned through your teaching how uptight I am. How on earth can I get over this? I've been this way since childhood."

"In adulthood we have a second chance to adjust our personalities," I said. "We can relate to others with wiser principles. Maybe you can become more patient with your weakness."

"But that's just the problem. I'm terribly ashamed of any weaknesses, even though I know I have some."

"What are they?" I asked.

"Well, I always want things to be perfect, yet my own bedroom is always a mess. I get on people if they're one minute late, but I'm often late. I feel upset if my teachers miss work from illness, yet I get sick several times every year. Why do I have these contradictions?"

"Your bedroom, lateness and illnesses are simply expressions of your weakness compass point—occasions when you're not in charge and not perfectly composed. By learning to accept these things, you'll become more patient with yourself and others."

"I've never felt accepted by anyone, including God. I've always had to earn my way, to prove my worth."

"That's your problem. You've never felt the inspiration

of grace. Grace is God to the rescue. May I pray for the Lord to help you discover more of his love?"

She nodded her head. We ended the session in prayer.

In our second session I showed Cora a "realistic self-image" diagram, and asked her to think out loud about how it applied to her.

This I can never be, even if I break my mind, heart, body and spirit, and even if I sacrifice everything else along the way.

This I can become, with reasonable effort, because it lies within my genuine genetic, psychological and spiritual capability.

This I am right now, and can enjoy, appreciate and expand. By trusting God and being my real self, I can learn and grow.

Cora studied this figure and pointed to the top story called the *idealized image*. "This is where I live my life," she said. "I expect too much of myself and end up feeling like a failure."

"What are some of the ideals in your top story?"

"I should be a perfect mother. My children should never get rowdy or upset or embarrass me in public. My teachers should never have problems or disagree with my opinion. I should be a perfect wife. My husband should never be disappointed in me, which he constantly is."

"Any demands when it comes to you and God?"

"I should be a perfect Catholic. I should obey all the commandments, participate in the Eucharist every Sunday, and never sin."

"Is that a heavy load or what?" I asked.

"But isn't perfection the goal of life? Doesn't the Bible say to be perfect for God is perfect?"

"I always thought so too, until I looked more closely at what Jesus was saying. Instead of asking us to be perfect, he's really calling on us to be patient and loving, to be tolerant and understanding of weakness."

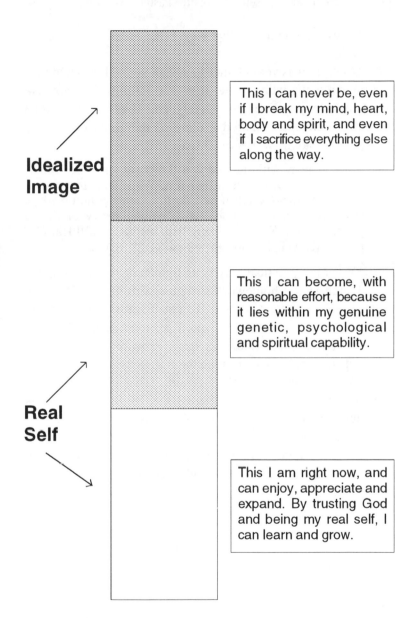

Idealized Image

This I can never be, even if I break my mind, heart, body and spirit, and even if I sacrifice everything else along the way.

This I can become, with reasonable effort, because it lies within my genuine genetic, psychological and spiritual capability.

Real Self

This I am right now, and can enjoy, appreciate and expand. By trusting God and being my real self, I can learn and grow.

REALISTIC SELF-IMAGE

"I never thought of it that way," she said, her body relaxing a little.

"Cora, now is your chance to accept yourself as an imperfect human being with normal fears and failings. Can you ask Jesus to help you live more freely and lightly?" I reached behind my chair and pulled a copy of the Bible out of my bookcase. I read the words of Christ:

> Get away with me and you'll recover your life. I'll show you how to take a real rest. Walk with me and work with me—watch how I do it. Learn the unforced rhythms of grace. I won't lay anything heavy or ill-fitting on you. Keep company with me and you'll learn to live freely and lightly (Matthew 11:28-30).[9]

"What is a practical way I can lighten up?" she asked.

I suggested a homework assignment to Cora. "Picture a scale from one to ten," I said. "Ten stands for perfection and one stands for failure. How do you judge most people?"

She smiled and shook her head. "I want them all to be tens, but since nobody is, I judge them as ones."

"That's what I thought," I said. "That's why you feel superior in relationships. So here's the growth stretch: this week tell yourself that if people make an average score of five, you'll accept them."

"So I'm supposed to respect mediocrity?" she exclaimed.

"How about being kind and accepting—like Jesus," I suggested.

A week later Cora came to our session with a notepad in her hand. She had kept tabs on the homework assignment. "I've become aware of how judgmental I actually am," she said. "It's appalling."

"Remember," I said, "be patient with yourself. How did you experience your criticalness versus your kindness?"

"I caught myself judging people constantly, but when I finally lowered my standards, I felt more accepting."

"That's progress," I said. "Keep exercising your love and weakness compass points until your strength is balanced by humble caring."

Over the next few months, Cora began using her love compass point to cheer people up, forgive more easily and feel emotionally connected to those around her. When she needed to assert herself, she did so with greater sensitivity to others' feelings. Though it was difficult, she learned to admit weaknesses without feeling humiliated. Her strength shifted from a compulsion to control others to an ability to cooperate with them. Her compass of the self was finally working.

The Controlling Pattern

Controllers are usually too self-sufficient to ask for help when they need it, too proud to say they are sorry, too competitive to be intimate and too self-centered to listen to others' needs. Exaggerated strength without the balance of weakness and love turns people into control freaks who use power to judge others.

The following symptoms can alert counselors to a controller's personality pattern:

1. They believe that there is only one way to do things: *their* way. They judge and reject anyone or anything that doesn't comply with their standards. Their need for perfection interferes with their ability to grasp the bigger picture. They are closed-minded but convinced that they know it all. They feel entitled to be "junior gods."

2. They are formal in manner, stiff in carriage and proper in conversation. Their relationships reflect a tense and serious quality, even at home with family members.

3. They derive inordinate pleasure from classifying

and managing things and people. They hoard worn-out or worthless objects. They are stingy but like to appear generous.

4. They usually opt for the dominant role in their families. Their constant need to talk down to others can make their spouses feel like children and their teenagers like little boys and girls.

5. They avoid the weakness and love poles of personality. Their consuming need is to give a good impression and to be in control at all times. Their Rock-of-Gibraltar self-image is paramount. This keeps them from laughing, playing, feeling, risking, sharing and learning.

6. They lack imagination and creativity. They rely on tradition or the rule book to prescribe what "should" be done in the present. They live mechanically by rite, ritual and propriety. They pooh-pooh feelings and consider introspection to be self-indulgent. They are often oblivious to their own and others' emotions.

7. They secretly strive for recognition and admiration. Their fundamental attitude is: "Strive at all times to demonstrate your strength and superiority." They view most other people as irresponsible, self-indulgent, lazy, incompetent and imperfect.

8. They view God as a figure of judgment and perfection who demands conformity and punishes individuality. Discipline and self-control are required at all times. They feel that God does not live or move outside of religious rules and regulations; that he does not speak outside the voice of tradition; that the dictates of authority must be obeyed to the letter of the law. They serve God through a demonstration of moral perfection and the ongoing correction of others.

Tips for Counseling Controllers

Controllers make for an interesting paradox in counseling, for they usually believe that they know more than the counselor. Their personality pattern resists growth. They lack the basic humility that would give them teachable spirits.

Controllers need to sense that you as the counselor know what you are doing. You need to be organized, in charge and insightful. For this reason, I often show controllers the master chart of compass counseling (see Appendix I) during their first session. This builds their confidence in the scientific underpinnings of personality theory.

Most controllers are analytical thinkers who repress their emotions, bodily sensations and spiritual sensitivity. Therefore, the best way to reach them is through their minds—through an appeal to logic. Real progress is made whenever controllers express feelings, disclose weakness or pray from their hearts.

As counselors we need to give controllers plenty of growth stretches for their hearts, bodies and spirits. Controllers must learn to experience, identify and handle love, anger, guilt and anxiety. They need to have patience with the feelings of others.

In the physical realm, controllers need to relax the body and enjoy it more. They have lived so exclusively in their minds that they need to enjoy a pleasant moment, melt their muscles in a luxurious bath, become more playful and enjoy their sex lives if they are married. By "loosing their minds and coming to their senses," the world becomes a brighter place. They break free from the black and white confines of controlling thoughts.

In the spiritual realm, controllers usually prefer stiff and formal relationships with God based on ritualized routine. We can encourage them toward greater intimacy with God—pouring out their feelings directly to him and actively trusting the Holy Spirit to help them.

Counseling Growth Stretches

1. Encourage them to honestly confess to the Lord that they desire a transforming experience of his love and grace. They can ask the Holy Spirit to help them fall in love with Jesus.

Suggest they laugh at their mistakes, let their schedules slide if it means helping someone else, and talk openly about their desires to be joyous or free.

2. Have them practice complimenting others' accomplishments. Remind them to bite their tongue when they start to qualify a compliment with some improvement that others need to make.

Help them practice building people up. They need to discover that they are not diminished when someone else succeeds. Suggest they offer support, encouragement and kind words, and quit being so righteously self-centered.

3. Advise them to honestly integrate people's constructive inputs. Recommend that they ask for feedback from friends and loved ones. Are they compulsive to a fault? Would they be liked better if they didn't pretend to know everything? Is it true that they are tense, grim and nit-picky? Can they refrain from arguing or defending themselves?

4. Suggest that they type out these Scriptures and put copies on their bathroom mirror or desktop. Have them ask God to help them hang loose and form a more relaxed reliance upon him.

> *Romans 14:10:* Why do you pass judgment on your brother or sister? Or you, why do you despise your brother or sister? For we will all stand before the judgment seat of God.

Luke 6:41, 42: Why do you see the speck in your neighbor's eye, but do not notice the log in your own eye?... You hypocrite, first take the log out of your own eye, and then you will see clearly to take the speck out of your neighbor's eye.

1 Peter 5:6-7: Humble yourselves therefore under the mighty hand of God, so that he may exalt you in due time. Cast all your anxiety on him, because he cares for you.

Romans 12:16: Live in harmony with one another; do not be haughty, but associate with the lowly.

2 Corinthians 12:9, 10: I will boast all the more gladly of my weaknesses, so that the power of Christ may dwell in me...for whenever I am weak, then am I strong.

1 Peter 5:6: Humble yourselves therefore under the mighty hand of God, so that he may exalt you in due time.

Psalm 51:17: The sacrifice acceptable to God is a broken spirit; a broken and contrite heart, O God, you will not despise.

Matthew 11:28-30: Come to me, all you that are weary and are carrying heavy burdens, and I will give you rest. Take my yoke upon you, and learn from me; for I am gentle and humble in heart, and you will find rest for your souls. For my yoke is easy, and my burden is light.

5. Suggest that between sessions they do three things that are frivolous and spontaneous. Some ideas? To go ride on a park swing, give someone an African violet, give their spouse a massage, buy a family game, wear a non-traditional outfit, go to lunch with the gang or take a day off and loaf.

Help them realize that the world doesn't rest on their shoulders. The best contributions they can make have to do with being warm, spontaneous and accepting of people.

Positives of the Strength Compass Point

Strength means a sense of adequacy and self-esteem. Strength is the inner affirmation that life is worth living. To feel good about competencies is neither sinful nor selfish. Without *self*-esteem counselees cannot esteem anyone else. Without strength they can never make a contribution. Strength enables people to be original and to bring their unique talents into the world.

The healthy expression of the strength compass point means saying, "I am adequate," "I am competent," "My life counts," and "I can contribute and cooperate."

Healthy strength uses power to benefit others, rather than judging and criticizing them. Maturity on the strength compass point can be tested by such questions as these:

• Can I be competent without being cocky?

• Do I use my confidence to cooperate with others, or to boss and dictate?

• Can I feel good about my strengths without judging others as less worthy than me?

• Can I make my own best efforts and ask for help when I need it?

The virtue of dignity arises from the strength pole. Human beings need to experience and express a sense of worth and confidence. We can follow many pathways to authentic strength, but the simplest one is by self-definition: "I am an adequate human being. I don't need to act superior. I can be myself and accept other people as they are. We are all God's children."

Eight

Releasing Resentment

S ome of the most difficult counseling sessions occur when counselees are caught in the grip of emotions such as resentment, guilt or depression. A good counselor needs a repertoire of techniques to transform these strongly negative feelings into therapeutic growth and gain.

When I went through my doctoral program to become a clinical psychologist, I found out that my personality was out of balance. I had never faced my aggressive tendencies.

Doctoral candidates were required to receive one hundred hours of psychotherapy before graduation. Looking back, I believe this was an excellent idea. It is unwise to counsel others without working through our own inner conflicts.

I felt awkward working with my first counselor, Dr. Vandenheuval. This distinguished, soft-spoken gentleman had white streaks of hair near his temples and smoked a pipe. He let me talk about myself for two full sessions.

At the end of the second session, I thought we were done. I tried to sum things up. "So, Dr. Vandenheuval, as you can see, I'm here on a mission from God and I hope to heal many disturbed people in my lifetime."

Calmly, the doctor blew a smoke ring into the air. "Dan," he said, "I admire your desire to help people. But I'm wondering when you're going to deal with the undercurrent of hostility in your personality."

I felt stunned beyond belief. I had thought I was going to leave his office with a clean bill of health. Here he was telling me that I was filled with resentment.

"I'm not angry at anybody!" I practically shouted.

"Then why are your fists clenched right now?" he asked, his eyes twinkling.

I looked down and saw the whites of my knuckles. I took a breath and eased myself back into the leather chair. *I really do need counseling*, I thought. In the ten minutes we had left, I told Dr. Vandenheuval about the violent town I'd grown up in and how I had become aggressive in order to survive.

He reached out his hand toward me. "Shake," he said. "You've just expressed something from your heart. Most of what you've said these last two sessions was B.S. So let's start next time with the anxiety and anger you felt growing up. Then we'll understand how it affects you today, and we'll find ways to get it out of your system."

In the next few sessions I felt greatly relieved talking about the past events that had tormented me. But, as the good doctor pointed out, talking isn't always enough.

During one session I described a time during my sophomore year in high school when a huge boy named Morris had jumped me. As I related the incident, adrenalin poured into my body and my heart raced. *It's incredible how this still affects me so powerfully*, I thought.

I spoke of how Morris had shoved me from behind, knocked me off my feet and sat down on my chest. He pounded my face mercilessly. His legs pinned down my arms, so I couldn't ward off the terrible blows.

Dr. Vandenheuval listened with great empathy. Then he

said, "How did you feel while you were trapped underneath the boy?"

"I felt terrified," I said, "and ashamed that he'd gotten the best of me." Just voicing those feelings loosened their grip on me.

The hostility that's trapped inside you is like a reservoir with too much water pressure. Muscular action will help drain it off.

"And what did you feel underneath the fear and shame?" he asked. "What did you want to do that you couldn't do at the time?"

Suddenly a dam burst inside me and a flood of hostility poured through. "I wanted to whack him upside the head, bloody his nose, push him off and beat him up!" I said, half shouting and half crying.

Dr. Vandenheuval opened his desk drawer and took out a towel. "Here, Dan, twist this towel as hard as you can. This isn't practice for hurting someone. It's a safe way to vent your anger and tell Morris whatever you want. The hostility that's trapped inside you is like a reservoir with too much water pressure. Muscular action will help drain it off."

I took the towel and squeezed it as hard as I could for about five minutes. I let out a stream of grunts that sounded like I was reliving the fight.

"In your mind's eye," he said, "let the situation turn out in your favor. Your unconscious needs to know that if you'd had a better break, you could have stood up for yourself. End the scene so that your dignity is intact."

I did as he said. I wrung out the towel several more times,

picturing myself standing up to Morris and holding my own. I began to feel a wonderful sense of relief. I realized that I am a worthwhile human being who can stand up for myself when I need to. But even when a situation temporarily overwhelms me, I don't need to feel ashamed. Over time, the undercurrent of hostility that Dr. Vandenheuval had spotted melted away.

Towel squeezing is a safe way for counselees to vent resentment and hostility. The counselor needs to clearly state: "Squeezing the towel is not practice for hurting or harming another human being. It simply provides a safe way to drain the reservoir of anger out of your personality."

What are some other ways of helping counselees safely release their resentment?

Direct Confrontation

Rita was an alcoholic by the age of twenty-five. Though her dependent personality pattern made her overly nice to those around her, when she drank she became explosive and vindictive. One time she had thrown her kitchen appliances out the window and cursed the police officers who came to investigate the disturbance.

After our first session, I admitted to her that psychological insight alone would not free her from her alcoholic rages. I suggested that if she'd agree to attend thirty Alcoholics Anonymous meetings in thirty days, therapy would be much more effective. Fortunately, this young woman was motivated to go to any lengths to improve her quality of life. She began attending AA that week.

When working with addictions, it is best to encourage the counselee to join a Twelve-Step group, since counseling alone is relatively ineffective in breaking the pattern of substance abuse.

Rita received a thirty-day chip a month later. Her ability to face her pent-up anger significantly increased.

In a fifth session, I asked her to recall her earliest childhood memories. I suspected that her inner pain began long ago.

"I'm in my crib—about two years old, I think. Daddy has come in again. He's putting something in my mouth and telling me to take Daddy's milk."

"What is he putting in your mouth?" I asked.

"It's long and warm and makes me gag. I try to spit it out but he won't let me. Then there's something like gooey, sticky stuff in my throat and he goes away."

"Was he putting his penis in your mouth?" I asked.

She exploded into tears. "Yes...yes...he kept doing that to me and I didn't know how to make him stop! It was awful."

"If this is accurate, your father was sexually molesting you," I said. But I needed more evidence to know that these memories were historically accurate. "Do you have any other memories at an older age?"

"Yes. When I was a little girl—clear up to about eight years old—he took video pictures of me naked and tried to French kiss me several times. I ran around the room so that he couldn't touch me."

"Where was your mother in all this?" I asked.

"I tried to tell her once when I was about seven because I felt so confused. But when I mentioned that Daddy had made me get naked, she slapped my face and called me a liar."

A case like this takes a lot of sorting through. Once the fact of sexual abuse was established, I made it clear to Rita that she was not at fault. I helped her feel accepted and respected for all the pain she'd been through.

Some time later, after Rita had worked through the shame that had plagued her for years, I used the towel squeezing technique to mobilize and release her rage. This prepared us for the final important step in her recovery—a face to face confrontation with her father.

Resentment can be released through role playing or direct

confrontation. Rita chose to fly to another state where her father was a hospital patient. She wanted to tell him how she felt about her childhood abuse. When Rita came back, she described what had happened:

> I walked into my father's hospital room feeling that God was going to help me be honest. I also heard your voice within me, Dr. Montgomery, spurring me forward. Daddy looked old and tired. His medications made him dull, but when I said that I wanted to talk about his sexual abuse, he perked right up.
>
> I said, "Daddy, I really resent how you used me as a sexual object and left me in the dark about what happened. You exploited me and ruined my trust in men, and you never even asked for forgiveness. I started drinking at thirteen to get rid of the awful feeling inside me. Now I know that my alcoholic rages really had your name on them."
>
> Daddy looked like he'd been hit on the head with a mallet. I guess he never expected me to talk about what he'd done. I prayed for God to help me. Then Daddy reached out for my hand and started crying. He said he'd hated himself all these years because he knew what he did was wrong. He said he was glad I'd come to talk to him. He said he might die soon, but he didn't want the abuse on his conscience anymore. He asked if I could forgive him, and suddenly, to my surprise, I knew I could.
>
> I realized as I left the hospital that this was the most courageous thing I'd ever done. I felt like Jesus had his arm around me as I walked away. I'm so glad I did this because Daddy died two weeks later.

Laying Aside Our Anger

It is not always feasible for our counselees to directly express their resentment. Perhaps the other person is no longer available or such a confrontation would only subject our counselees to further abuse. Even so, we can help them to symbolically lay down their burden of anger.

I worked with Katrina who was thirty-years-old. She came into therapy carrying resentment toward her ex-husband who had divorced her and moved to another state. I empathized with Katrina's hurt, but asked if she wanted to be done with her anger. She said that she wanted to but didn't know how.

A stack of cedar logs lay by the fireplace next to my desk. I told Katrina to pick up three logs and stand in front of me. As she did so, I talked about how carrying around a load of anger is grim and exhausting. After five minutes of holding the logs, her arms shook and ached with pain. I just kept talking. Finally, Katrina cried out, "I can't hold this wood any longer! Can I please put it down?"

"That's a great idea," I said. "Here, I'll help you."

I took my time lifting each log out of her arms. She breathed more easily as her load lightened. With the last log lifted, the pain left and she felt nothing but relief.

Katrina broke into a smile. "You mean that's what I can do with my anger? Put it down?"

"How much longer do you want to carry it?" I asked.

Katrina collapsed into the chair. Her shoulders slackened. She heaved a sigh. After a minute or two, she looked at me with clear eyes. "I just laid down my anger toward Russell. I don't need it anymore." The peaceful look on her face convinced me that Katrina meant what she said.

Counselors can use this same exercise with a stack of books from their bookshelves. The key for success is to make sure that the counselee wants to lay down the burden of anger and is willing to let bygones be bygones. In some instances, several sessions are required to help a counselee lay aside resentment. As counselees face and work through their anger, a burden is relieved and they feel more relaxed with God and others.

Nine

Getting Rid of Guilt

The blue sky soared above the towering brown canyon walls of the Rio Grande gorge, which kept my six-year-old eyes spellbound. My father parked the car at the end of the long winding dirt road beside the Rio Grande, a legendary river known for its beauty and treacherous depths.

I sprang from the car and raced to the river's edge. My dog Blackie barked at my heels. Mom carried her red picnic basket to a nearby table. Daddy unpacked his fishing tackle from the car trunk.

"Danny," came my Dad's voice from behind me. "Don't get so close to the water. It's ten or twenty feet deep out from the bank. You and Blackie play over by the picnic table."

I kicked a reddish rock off the bank and watched the hungry current devour it. Blackie darted after a yellow butterfly and I danced after him a dozen feet downstream. There, the tops of two huge boulders jutted temptingly out from a deep pool.

I glanced back at Daddy. His head was turned downward as he tied a trout fly to his fishing line. Mom was spreading out a table cloth. A naughty feeling shimmied up through my belly. "I'm a good jumper," I said to Blackie. "Wanna see?"

Up into the air I leapt, coming down on the first big boulder. My heart beat proudly with success. *That was easy*, I thought.

I sized up the distance to the second boulder—about two or three feet—bent my knees and leap-frogged once more. My jump fell short, my feet cutting through the icy water like a knife. The blue sky and canyon walls disappeared from view. I saw green bubbles all around me. A thunderous silence filled my ears. Gulping in water, my lungs burned like fire.

I was sinking like a rock when something powerful gripped the floating strands of my hair. A sharp tug reversed my motion. Up I came until the colors of sky and canyon burst into my vision.

Dad hauled me up out of the river. His voice exploded in my ear, "I got 'im Anna Mae!" I found out later that he had bolted to the boulder where I'd vanished and shot his long muscular arm down into the watery depths. He'd anchored his fingers into my hair, and snatched me back from the icy jaws of death.

I coughed water out of my nose and mouth. Mom wrapped my shivering body in a blanket from the car. Blackie paced nervously back and forth, his eyes glued on me. Once I got my breath, I cried with all my might.

But the next thing that happened scared me worse than the near drowning. "Danny," my irate father yelled, "why'd you disobey me? Why did you go out on that rock when I told you to stay by your mother?"

At that moment I knew I had blown it. My stomach churned. I felt too guilty to offer an answer for myself. But within moments another part of me gave Dad a plausible excuse. "Blackie pushed me!" I lied.

Build a Bridge of Rapport

Counselees sometimes avoid responsibility for their actions and turn a deaf ear to their conscience by blaming someone and excusing themselves—just as I blamed Blackie in order to excuse myself to my father. Rationalization is a well known way of escaping detection for misbehavior, but this defense mechanism never leads to growth. Counseling must disarm it.

The *Catechism* says: "It is important for every person to be sufficiently present to himself in order to hear and follow the voice of his conscience. This requirement of *interiority* is all the more necessary as life often distracts us from any reflection, self-examination or introspection" (n. 1779).[10]

A good way to help counselees examine themselves is to disclose one of our own character defects. Counselees feel relieved when their counselor admits to being fully human.

A judge sent me a sixteen-year-old boy named Eric. Over the weekend he had been caught breaking and entering. Seeing me was his alternative to facing charges.

Eric took a seat in my office and glared at me.

"Hey, dude, they really busted you, didn't they?" I said.

He grunted, nodding.

"How did you screw up?"

He talked through his teeth. "Didn't count on the night watchman. Should've cased the place better. Stupid police came right away."

"Bummer," I said. "This your first job?"

"Yeah. I could 'a really scored."

"I'm smarter than you," I said with a wry grin.

"You're what?" he asked, shifting in his seat.

"I'm smarter than you. When I was your age, I always posted a watch down the block when I stole hub caps off cars. I'd hear a whistle if a black and white cruised by."

"Really?" He broke into a smile. "Cool. I never thought of that."

Now we were off and running. Eric crossed the bridge of rapport I'd offered him. He opened up, not just about the heist, but about his frustrations with life.

At the end of the session I said, "Eric, I really like you. I think I know a way out of this mess."

"What?" he asked.

"Why don't you go down to the police station tomorrow? Ask for the captain. Tell him you're really sorry for the break-in and you want to make amends."

"Make amends?"

"Yeah. Paint the police station or something that will benefit other people."

"Why should I do that?" he asked.

"You're guilty of breaking and entering, aren't you?"

"Yeah."

"So this is a way to wipe the slate clean. Start over. The way I see it you have a choice here. Either you're going to choose the road to jail or you're going to get your act together and make something better of yourself. I faced this same choice. I'm glad I decided to become a psychologist instead of a thief. It's a lot more fun."

At our next session, Eric proudly announced that over the next six weekends he was going to paint the entire police building. At the end of that time his offense would be taken off his record.

The Courage of Imperfection

When counselees feel guilt, they reflexively cover up to avoid the humiliation that comes from acknowledging their imperfections. They try to shield themselves from the logical consequences of their actions. They create the illusion that the world—not themselves—needs correction. But this tactic backfires. Their guilt remains, festering in their souls.

As compass counselors, we can model and teach the *courage of imperfection*. Guilt arising from wrongdoing or failure is a normal part of life. St. John writes: "If we say that we have no sin, we deceive ourselves, and the truth is not in us. If we confess our sins, he who is faithful and just will forgive us our sins and cleanse us from all unrighteousness" (1 John 1:8-9).

Guilt is a temporary movement into the weakness compass point, where we do the necessary soul-searching to mend our ways. By exercising the courage of imperfection, our counselees fulfill the age-old challenge issued by St. Augustine in the fourth century: "Return to your conscience, question it.... Turn inward, brethren, and in everything you do, see God as your witness" *(Commentary on the Epistle of John).*

We can help counselees confess their guilt without shaming them, since the fear of humiliation is one of the biggest barriers to honest confession. While we don't brook counselees' efforts to rationalize or cloak their misdeeds, we are quick to show admiration for the courage to come clean. As soon as counselees feel and face their guilt, we focus on how they can make amends.

The Three-Minute Guilt Trip

Authentic guilt is an important ingredient for counselees' mental and spiritual health. Healthy guilt is triggered when counselees have harmed someone, been untrue to themselves or gone against God's loving nature. Shame is a wake-up call from the Holy Spirit, encouraging our counselees to make things right. "The confession (or disclosure) of sins," declares the *Catechism*, "even from a simply human point of view, frees us and facilitates our reconciliation with others" (n. 1455).[11]

So when counselees have blown it, tell them to concentrate on the feeling of guilt for three full minutes. Reassure them that there is no need to be morbid or to condemn themselves forever. They can accept the guilt feeling, make a conscious apology to God and talk over their plans to make amends.

One woman named Francine felt guilty for ten years because she'd had a habit of stealing items from her grocery store. In my office she concentrated on the guilt for three minutes. Then a smile crept over her face.

"I've asked God to forgive me," she said, "and I'm going to put extra items back on the shelves for the next year." During the following year Francine bought more groceries than she needed, replacing several items on the shelves each week until her debt was paid.

Reworking a Past Event

Mildred, a seventy-year-old woman with dependent tendencies, had been grieving over the loss of her husband for two years. She felt guilty because she hadn't been with him at the moment of his death.

"I'll just never forgive myself for not being by his side when he died," she sighed.

"Where were you?" I asked.

"I'd been with him day and night for three days. On the evening he died I had to use the restroom. He was in intensive care and there was no restroom in his room. I walked down the hall to the ladies room. He was dozing when I left. When I got back a few minutes later he was dead." At this, she broke down and sobbed for several minutes.

I sensed that just listening to her wasn't going to resolve this problem. I needed a way to catapult Mildred out of the weakness compass point and into her strength so as to restore her dignity.

I waited until she dabbed her eyes with a Kleenex and regained her composure. As a prelude to moving into the technique I had in mind, I reflected the feeling she'd just expressed.

"Mildred, it seems unforgivable to you that you weren't there for him. You'd been his faithful companion for forty years of marriage, and now from your view, when he needed you most, you abandoned him."

"That's right, Dr. Dan. That's why I can never forgive myself."

"All right," I said. "Let's replay the events of that night." I pointed to the sofa in my office. "Pretend that the sofa is the hospital bed." I propped up two sofa pillows on one end. "These pillows represent your husband."

"What am I supposed to do?" she asked.

"I want you to pull your chair up next to him. Tell him what happened that night and how awful you've felt about it for two years."

"I don't think I can do this—talk to him, I mean."

"It's easier than you think. Tell me what he's wearing tonight."

She looked toward the sofa. "He's got on his blue polka-dot flannel pajamas. I had to have special permission for him to wear them."

I helped her move her chair next to the sofa. I noticed that her gaze had turned tender. "Go ahead," I said. "In this role play you're allowed to spend a few brief minutes with him. Say anything you want."

"Hi Dean," she said, a catch in her voice. "I know you just need to sleep and get your rest. But I've got to tell you that I didn't mean to leave you when you died." She started to choke up, but cleared her throat and continued. "I stayed with you day and night for three days. You probably don't remember because you were doped up. The doctor didn't know you were going to die that night. Things seemed pretty normal. It was eight o'clock when I had to go to the restroom." She looked at me for reassurance.

"You're doing fine," I said. "Go on."

"Well, honey, I just took a few minutes, but when I came back you were gone." She sighed deeply.

"What is he saying back?" I asked.

She turned to me. "He says he understands. That everybody has to go to the bathroom and it's not a big deal."

"What else?"

She looked toward the sofa and a little smile came over her face. "He says that I'm being too hard on myself, just like I always was. He says I should lighten up."

"So he forgives you for not being there?" I asked.

"Oh sure. He says he went to be with God that night and knew that even though I was in the bathroom, I loved him with all my heart."

"How do you feel right now?"

"I feel warm all over. I feel Dean's love."

"Okay, take one more minute and say any last words. These are the words you would have said if you'd been with him."

She blew her nose into a Kleenex and took a deep breath. "I feel so much better now, Dean. You always did know how to make me smile. Thanks for understanding what happened that night. I've got to go now. I'll always love you. Bye bye."

Ten

Dealing with Depression

M ost counselees feel depressed when they come to us. No matter which compass point they normally favor, depression creates a temporary sense of helplessness and failure that sends them into the weakness compass point.

For people who are too controlling or too aggressive, this is a blessing in disguise. Experiencing temporary weakness helps them reach out to God and others. For counselees who are too dependent or too withdrawn, depression gives them a chance to get a grip on life, to take active stands for recovery, and to marshal the courage of self-determination.

While there are psychological and spiritual causes for depression, a number of counselees suffer from a biological depression that has never been correctly diagnosed.

Biological Causes of Depression

Biological depression results when a counselee's body doesn't produce enough catecholamine molecules, or neurotransmitters, for the billions of synapses in the nervous system. These molecules work directly to transmit bioelectrical impulses between all nerve cells.

How does a chronic deficiency of neurotransmitters affect the behavior of such counselees? Their thinking gets muddled. They feel down in the dumps. Their bodies are easily fatigued. Lacking energy to fire up the nervous system to normal functioning, they can't cope with daily stress. The slightest problem, such as an unpaid bill, seems like a major catastrophe.

Here are eight clinical signs that reveal biological depression:

- *Loss of pleasure* in activities which normally bring satisfaction

- A *haunting fatigue* that isn't relieved by sleep; a lack of follow-through in getting things done

- *Erratic sleeping patterns* such as insomnia, fitful sleeping or early morning wakening

- *Decreased love and affection* to the point of feeling indifferent toward friends and family members

- *Indecisiveness* about even the simplest matters

- *Anxiety* in the form of tension, fear or irritability

- *Vague and unpleasant sensations* in the chest, stomach and/or solar plexus—an ominous "dark" or "blue" feeling

- *Suicidal thoughts*

When several of these symptoms persist over a period of months or years, this strongly indicates biological depression. An anti-depressant may be needed. Anti-depressants provide the body with sufficient neurotransmitters to bring the brain and nervous system up to par. The dark mood lifts. The depressed person becomes free to think more clearly, feel more vividly and relax more easily.

If counselees are near-sighted or far-sighted, they need glasses. If they are diabetic, they need insulin. And if they suffer from biological depression, they need an anti-depressant. Anti-depressants are non-addictive, anti-stress agents which—when properly prescribed—enhance the quality of life.

I suggest that counselors form a therapeutic alliance with a psychiatrist who is knowledgeable about anti-depressants. A psychiatrist can make a medical evaluation of counselees who remain depressed despite good counseling. Once stabilized on the medication, counselees become much more amenable to the counseling process.

It is important not to judge biochemical depression as a moral lapse of faith or a negative attitude about life. Counselees who need and receive an anti-depressant usually report that their energy has improved and their mood is more positive within three weeks.

Biological Depression and Addiction

Many biologically depressed counselees secretly try to medicate themselves with substances such as food, alcohol, nicotine, marijuana or cocaine. These substances provide a short term high, while depressing the nervous system even further. Addiction substantially deepens depression.

Harry was a gifted surgeon in a state of crisis at the age of forty-five because he couldn't develop a lasting relationship with a woman. His latest attempt in a one-year-old relationship was bordering on catastrophe.

Harry told me how depressed he felt about the relationship. I used a number of therapeutic techniques to calm his tensions and increase his male/female communication skills. After three months he had experienced little improvement. Finally I said, "Harry, there must be something in the equation that you're not telling me. You're still tense and anxious, but we should be seeing progress by now. What are you holding back from me?"

Harry blushed. "Well, Dr. Dan, I guess I've never mentioned a few minor things." These "few minor things" turned out to be his daily intake of six gin and tonics, three packs of cigarettes and twenty-five cups of coffee.

"Harry, you're creating physiological chaos in your body. Alcohol creates depression. Nicotine creates stress. Coffee creates anxiety. These are all systemic poisons. If you keep this up, you'll solve your depression about women in the most drastic way—*by dying*. We need to work on getting you substance-free so that you can enjoy life instead of killing yourself."

Harry retorted with a classic answer: "But I have to have these little indulgences! I'm too depressed!"

At my suggestion, Harry joined Alcoholics Anonymous. For a medical evaluation of his depression, he agreed to see a psychiatrist. As soon as Harry joined AA and had taken an anti-depressant for a month, his mood stabilized. His new concentration allowed him to assimilate what I'd been teaching him about how to conduct a healthy man/woman relationship. Harry now has a good marriage and remains sober. He's still attending AA.

Whether the origins of depression are biological or psychological, counselees need psychological strategies for changing their learned patterns of depressed behavior.

Psychological Causes of Depression

Psychological depression develops in people who keep their inner lives to themselves. *De*pression is the opposite of *ex*pression. Psychologist Sidney Jourard suggests that people often need counseling "because they have not disclosed themselves in some optimal degree to the people in their life."[12]

When counselees do not disclose their inner lives to others, they are left shut-up unto themselves—like corked bottles drifting aimlessly at sea. Soren Kierkegaard coined the phrase "shut-upness" to describe the malady of depression that comes from social isolation.

How is depression transformed into vibrant self-expression? The word *de-pression* implies that one's inner life with all its potential richness and grace is *pressed down* out of awareness.

To illustrate this notion, I sometimes stand in front of seated counselees and place my hands on their shoulders, gently pushing downward.

"The downward pressure that you now feel," I say, "is like the depression that haunts you. As long as I push down on your shoulders, you will feel heavy, helpless and unable to move freely in the world. If I push hard enough, you won't even be able to stand up. You'll feel trapped."

Counselees agree that the sensation of feeling trapped in the chair is like living in the grip of depression. Then they can more easily recognize how they create their own depression by pushing their feelings out of awareness.

Suppressing Feelings

Suppression is the mildest form of pushing feelings out of awareness. Depressed counselees *su*ppress too much of their originality.

Suppression isn't all bad. It is healthy to temporarily suppress an emotion. This is called impulse control and allows people to decide whether or not it's appropriate to express themselves in certain situations. Healthy people may suppress a feeling while still remaining aware of it. They choose another time for self-expression. Depressed counselees, however, suppress feelings indiscriminately and lose touch with themselves.

If suppression persists as a personal tendency, then repression—a more severe and permanent form of suppression—soon follows.

Repressing Feelings

Repression means that vital emotions are stuffed into the unconscious, and are no longer available to conscious awareness. When role-playing the effects of repression, push down hard and firmly on counselees' shoulders, making it difficult for them to breathe or move. This is exactly how a severely depressed person feels.

An ongoing pattern of repression causes feelings to fester inside counselees, creating sensations of physical tension, psychological discontent and spiritual malaise. Being out of touch with themselves leaves them feeling disconnected from others and God.

Emotional repression leaves counselees in the dark about who they are and what they need from life. Repression, then, blocks the *ex*pression of identity and intimacy with others.

A male counselee who was a construction worker put it this way:

> For years I didn't allow myself to feel hurt, sadness or anger. I wouldn't even acknowledge to myself that I felt bad. I overate constantly to avoid the pain. Depression stepped in big time to the point of my wanting not to live anymore.
>
> I learned in compass counseling how to express my feelings for the first time. Now I know what I'm feeling, and it doesn't take me long to figure out why. I now share some of my inner life with my wife and my buddies at work.

Oppressed Feelings

A last form of emotional depression comes from *op*pression, and occurs when counselees live in an environment that undermines and opposes their freedom of expression. Ethnic or religious groups can be oppressed. Nations can be oppressed.

For many centuries women have been oppressed. Discrimination and ill-treatment—whether based on wealth, class, race, religion or gender—coerces victims to hide their feelings by suppression or repression in order to survive.

In counseling hundreds of couples, I've found that a common cause of depression in women are the fathers, boyfriends, husbands or sons who may dominate or exploit them. Denied the dignity of healthy self-expression, these women fall into seemingly inexplicable depression. Good counseling empowers them to stand up and confront an oppressive relationship instead of masochistically tolerating it.

On the other hand, men often become depressed because of boring or demeaning work situations in which their subjective inner life is sacrificed for a company or boss's profit quota. "True development," says the *Catechism,* "concerns the whole man. It is concerned with increasing each person's ability to respond to his vocation and hence to God" (n. 2461).[13] If depression persists because of employment conditions, it may be time to talk to a supervisor, negotiate for a better deal or even make a career change. These situations can be discussed and role-played in counseling before a counselee undertakes them.

Spiritual Causes of Depression

Some people are caught up in the Jonah Complex. Like the Old Testament prophet Jonah, they run away from their spiritual calling. Whether they are our counselees, students or parishioners, we can offer healing prayer to help them find spiritual renewal.

Twenty-four, intelligent, and handsome, Dave radiated confidence from having achieved his lifelong dream: being drafted by one of the teams in the National Football League. Soon afterward this young married man enrolled in one of my graduate psychology classes. I'd frequently notice him peering into the lobby mirror to recomb his hair and check out his appearance. His life seemed to center around the admiration won by his physique and football prowess.

But tragedy struck Dave an unexpected blow. The next semester he came down with hepatitis. We all felt concerned for him, and I arranged with his wife to pass along his assignments so that he wouldn't get too far behind.

A month later Dave returned to try to finish out the semester. A different man walked into the room. His spirit seemed shattered. He had lost weight. That afternoon his doctors had told him he could never play football again. On the way to class, Dave thought of ending his life by driving into a freeway embankment. He felt betrayed by life.

After class I invited Dave into my office to offer extra support. We talked for awhile. I suggested that there might be a deeper meaning to this calamity than met the eye. I asked him to think about what life might be asking of him. Still depressed, my struggling student left school for the day.

In class a day later Dave mused, "I'm beginning to think that I've lived too narrowly. All I ever thought about was my football career. Maybe life is telling me that's not enough. Maybe I can expand my horizons through this."

At the end of the semester, I invited Dave into my office one last time. The Lord seemed to impress me that Dave was now ready to face life on new terms. We talked a few minutes.

"I'm accepting the fact that my football career is over," he said. "But I need to find something else to get excited about. I think I need help from God."

I asked if he wanted me to pray with him. Dave said yes.

"Dear God," I prayed, "this disease was a terrible blow. Dave was about to play football in front of the world, and now he can never play again. Will you please bring new insights out of his pain? Can you help new goals to grow within him? We give his life to you, in Jesus' name."

Then I asked Dave to pray. After a long pause, he looked up sheepishly. "I don't know how," he admitted. "I've never prayed out loud before."

"Talk to God just like you're talking to me. Be honest. Tell him how you feel and what you need."

Dave took a deep breath and bowed his head. "I've made a mess out of things, God. I handled the hepatitis like a spoiled brat. When I didn't get my way I wanted to quit life. I'm sorry. I got so obnoxious that my wife hates me now. She's a great lady, God. Help me not to lose her. I've been such a jerk! Please help me change. Please guide my life." Dave's voice trembled with these last words.

I looked up. Tears welled up in his eyes, yet he was smiling. Dave looked right at me, eyes aflame with emotion. "Something is right here in this room. Something is all over me, Dan! Someone is touching me! Is it God?"

I also felt the Lord's presence around us. "Yes," I assured this young man. "God is pouring his love into you. Just relax and let it happen. I think your pain is being healed."

Dave put his hand over his heart. "I feel all warm inside. What do I do next?"

"Say 'Thank you,'" I suggested.

When Dave left my office that evening, his face beamed and his eyes shone. "Wow, man. I never knew God *really* answered prayer. Not like that! I'll stay in touch. Thanks for the course. Thanks for your prayers."

Dave invited me to lunch a few months later to tell me that he'd reconciled with his wife and accepted a high school coaching job for the following year. Gone was the pain and depression that had been etched into his face earlier in the year.

"I never knew I could feel this much peace in life," he said. "It started the night I asked God to take over and guide me."

Eleven

A Counselee's Image of God

A woman named Carolyn said with teary eyes, "I always wanted my dad to notice me and say I was pretty. But he only paid attention to my two older brothers and hardly ever spoke to me. I felt tiny and insignificant, like he didn't care that I had been born. I realized in counseling that I feel the same way about God—I'm afraid he doesn't care that I exist."

Counselees' experiences with their parents play a crucial role in forming their inner image of God. By understanding this we can help them shed faulty images of God and experience more of his grace and glory. A balanced image of God always enhances counseling and strengthens our counselees' personality and spiritual health.

When I asked Carolyn about her image of God, she said, "I've always longed to be close to God, but deep inside I feel like he doesn't have time for me."

Here are some questions you can ask your counselees in order to help clarify their inner image of God:

- Did you admire or fear your parents? Did you love or hate them?

• Did your parents laugh and play with you, and talk to you about life?

• Did they overly control or constantly criticize you?

• Were you the recipient of verbal abuse or cruel punishment from your parents?

• Did you feel neglected or abandoned?

• How do you feel toward your parents today?

• What is your image of God?

• What is the most frequent gut feeling that you experience when you think about God?

• How do you feel toward the Father, the Son and the Holy Spirit?

• How do you believe God feels toward you?

All people at first project their perception of the most emotionally significant parent onto God. How can counselees learn to withdraw this projection? How can they evolve a perception of God that fosters feelings of intimacy and trust? It is important to find out if counselees are stuck with dependent, aggressive, withdrawn or controlling images of God.

The Dependent Image

I learned much about the importance of the dependent image of God by counseling a woman named Anna Marie, who was referred to me by her priest.

Anna Marie came into my office looking flustered and breathless. A thirty-year-old woman, she had on a pale blue wool dress with a gray scarf tied tastefully around her neck. Minutes into our first session, teary mascara lines ran down onto her cheeks.

"I can't understand what's wrong with me," she cried.

"There's such a difference between the way people see me and the way I feel inside." She paused for a deep breath. "I love my kids and my husband. I'm very active in our church. I love the Lord. Why do I secretly think about ending my life? No one even knows how depressed I am."

———————❖———————

*The dependent image of God
ties a counselee to self-sacrifice
at the expense of self-realization in Christ.
But both are needed
for a balanced spiritual life.*

———————❖———————

"Do you have a feeling that you've got to take care of everyone around you, yet you end up feeling all alone?" I asked.

"That's it!" she exclaimed. "I feel responsible for making everyone happy, as if that's my mission in life."

"So you bend over backward helping other people," I reflected, "but no one ends up taking care of you. Have you neglected loving yourself?"

Anna Marie's brown eyes blinked and she cleared her throat. "Whenever I think about my own needs I feel guilty."

As I probed more deeply, I found that Anna Marie had grown up in an exceptionally devout religious home. Her father was a deacon who always helped anyone who was in need. She spoke of her father in glowing terms, describing him as a selfless man who lived for others.

I affirmed her father's admirable virtues, but wondered aloud if Anna Marie knew that loving others required taking good care of herself.

"But I can't stand the thought of disappointing anyone," she wailed. "Doesn't the Lord want me to meet everyone's needs without thinking of myself?"

During counseling sessions, Anna Marie began to understand Jesus' summary of a balanced life: "Love God with all your heart—and love others *as you love yourself.*" Slowly, she realized that she had left herself out of the equation. We talked about how she could care for her needs without feeling guilty, express her opinions honestly, say no to excessive demands on her time and energy, and follow her inner truth in Christ—all without running herself ragged trying to please everyone.

Her therapeutic breakthrough came the day she clearly stated, "I know now that God loves me and doesn't expect me to wait hand-and-foot on everybody. I've found out that people still like me, even though I express myself more and take stands about what I can and cannot do."

The dependent image of God ties a counselee to self-sacrifice at the expense of self-realization in Christ. But both are needed for a balanced spiritual life. Jesus epitomized the life of a humble servant, yet he unflinchingly expressed his feelings and followed the Father's will, not kowtowing to people's approval or disapproval.

The Aggressive Image

While some parents are humble and loving, others are mean and punitive. How do you counsel someone whose Mom or Dad was like this? Aggressive parents make their children walk on eggshells. They blame and attack their kids, even when they think they're trying to help them.

Counselees who had such a parent may turn out to be aggressive themselves, unconsciously seeing God as wrathful and harsh. Unfortunately, some Catholics suffer from the perception of a God who is out to punish them, or who uses them to inflict his punishment upon others.

A client named Michael sat before me with a defiant look on his face. He was wearing a blue and grey plaid shirt, faded blue jeans and leather work boots. He conveyed a strong, no-nonsense attitude. He'd stated on the phone that his wife said he mistreated her and had asked him to seek counseling. But once seated, he declared, "I'm not an abusive husband. I just want my family to obey me. If they don't, I get mad."

"What is the most recent example of you getting mad?" I asked.

"Well, yesterday I wanted my wife to hurry up and get in the car. But she ran back into the house to get some flowers she was going to drop off for someone. She took too long, so I stormed back into the house. I saw the flowers on the kitchen table and decided to teach her a lesson for holding me up. I tore the flowers to shreds and threw them on the floor. She went to pieces and said I needed counseling."

Over several sessions I found out that Michael had been raised in a very stern Catholic home. His father had often humiliated him as a boy, spanking him severely for minor infractions. Once Michael needed a new pair of shoes for walking through the mud to school. His old shoes had holes in them. When he asked his father for shoes, his dad lit into him, telling him he was a spoiled weakling.

Gradually, I helped Michael recognize that his father was an angry man who blamed and attacked people no matter what they did. It was hard for Michael to accept this truth because he viewed his father with god-like awe.

It was even harder for Michael to admit he was treating his wife with contempt, just like his father had treated Michael's mother. A breakthrough came when I asked Michael to describe his image of God.

"Well, Dr. Dan, I believe that God hates those who don't obey him totally. That's why I'm so hard on my wife and kids. I'm God's instrument for punishing them so they'll fear him."

"Michael," I said gently. "You're describing your own father!"

Over the next few months of counseling, Michael eased up his iron-fisted rule of his family. We practiced saying prayers of blessing together in therapy, so that he could say these same prayers over his wife and children.

Slowly, over six months of counseling, Michael relinquished his image of God as spiteful and aggressive. The Holy Spirit responded to our healing prayers, and this physically powerful man grew tender and malleable in the loving hands of his heavenly Father.

The Withdrawn Image

What happens if your counselee had a parent who was weak and indecisive—a parent who didn't pay any attention? Such an early childhood experience creates an unconscious image of God as a withdrawn Father. Counselees assume that God ignores them, goes back on his promises and doesn't really care that they exist. Even when these counselees experience major problems, they have trouble calling on God because they believe that he's not interested in helping them.

My own father, Charles, was an emotionally detached man who preferred a hermit-like existence. He had his work and his hobbies, but was oblivious to people—including me. My father's own dad and mom died when he was a little boy. Charles was raised without much supervision by his crippled aunt, who was a shut-in. He never learned how to relate emotionally to others, so he didn't know how to show love and affection.

As a child I often longed for Dad to get on the carpet and tickle me, or chuck a baseball in the yard or tell me he felt proud of me as his son. But Dad was a man of few words. I'm sure he loved me, but I don't think it ever occurred to him to say so, or to romp around with me in fun. He preferred to work in his den on solitary projects until the day he died.

Without knowing it, I believed for years that God was a remote and aloof Being who was absorbed in running the Milky Way or handling the affairs of the universe—but had no interest in a kid like me. Whenever someone mentioned God, I'd get an empty feeling in my belly.

By the age of seventeen my sense of loneliness had become excruciating. I didn't feel emotionally connected to anything or anybody. One day in church, I cried out in my heart to God. *If you exist, and if you really are loving, please show me*, I pleaded. When I went up and knelt at the altar, the minister must have sensed the gray cloud hanging over me. He put his hand on my shoulder and prayed for Christ to give me peace.

At that moment—with the ease of slipping on a velvet glove—I felt the peace of Jesus Christ blessing my soul with joyous love. That was thirty years ago. I am thankful that the image of my heavenly Father as tenderly caring has prevailed over the withdrawn image of God that dogged my footsteps in childhood.

The Controlling Image

Sometimes our counselee's experiences with a mother leaves a greater imprint on the psyche than does the father. In this case, the image of the mother is unconsciously projected onto God.

Natalie, a forty-year-old college professor with red hair and green eyes, sought counseling because of her feelings of estrangement from God. A competent wife, mother and educator, she was troubled that she could never establish a feeling of intimacy with God.

I suggested to her that I sensed a connection between her distrust of her mother and her distrust of God. At first she denied this, but gradually benefited from the insight. Here is a letter from her that describes her growth process.

For me, it was a fairly long process to my current friendship with God. During my childhood, my mother controlled my actions with a gruff stern voice, using withering retorts if I tried to stand up for myself. Being a sensitive child, it didn't take long for me to feel scared of her and intimidated by the bossy way in which she ran our home. My father was away often on business—so she controlled everything in my life.

Her shrill, carping voice sent chills down my spine. "Natalie, I'm going to examine your room in ten minutes and it had better be clean as a pin!" "Natalie, hurry up or you'll be late." "Natalie, can't you do anything right?" I always felt under the gun, as though she was glaring over my shoulder. Even in college and after I got married I felt this way.

Dr. Montgomery, when you asked if there was a connection between how I felt around my mother and how I felt toward God, I thought you were crazy. What could my mother possibly have to do with my image of God? And then the insight struck me like a thunderbolt. As a child I assumed that God was a superior, condescending judge—the very thought of him filled me with tension. I didn't want to get close to God because I assumed that he only wanted to control me, just like my mother!

In college I quit believing in a personal God. The universe ran on orderly principles which didn't need sentimental explanations such as the involvement of God. There was a ten-year period when I didn't utter a single prayer.

It wasn't until I came into therapy that I began to understand that a real friendship with God was even *possible*. In therapy you talked openly about your friendship with Jesus. I felt angry. You were insulting my intelligence by talking about a personal relationship with the Divinity. But I had to admit that we were getting good results in healing the wounds in my personal life, and that you weren't a kook. This made me consider what you were saying about God.

To be honest, I was envious. I wondered why God would talk to you and not to everybody around the world. Or maybe I just wasn't listening. The bottom line was that my fear of being controlled by God was keeping me from a close relationship with him.

Then a crisis came into my life. My fifteen-year-old daughter had a car accident and almost died in the emergency room. I got on my knees in the corridor and prayed for about an hour. A presence came over me that shifted me into another dimension of reality. I felt a peace and a clarity. The air around me seemed charged with love. I continued praying, but now with every part of my being.

The peace which descended on me that night has not left. I think that crisis cracked my shell. It drew out a greater love for my daughter than I had ever known. I felt willing to die for her. But it also helped me realize that God has that same love for me. I smiled later that week when God seemed to whisper that I had been a hard nut to crack.

I'd never suspected that my view of God had been contaminated by my experiences with my mother. But now that I've quit projecting her image onto the Lord, God's love accompanies me wherever I go!

The Revealed Image of God

Our counselees' experiences with their earthly parents shape their perception of God. A therapeutic relationship presents the opportunity to discuss and discard archaic and unconscious projections onto God. We help them develop a more mature and balanced image of God.

Here are some questions to explore with our counselees:

• Can you talk to God without being formal and religious? Do you share spontaneously throughout the day or do you censor what you believe God would find unacceptable?

• Can you talk to God about every topic without feeling self-conscious, or do you clam up on taboo topics even though you need help and guidance?

• Can you come out with whatever is in your heart without striving to appear nice, proper, moral and good? Or do you need to impress God with your purity, strength, propriety and character?

• Can you talk to God day and night wherever you are? Or do you feel that a church or holy place is the only place where you can commune with God?

• Can you be emotionally honest with God? Or do you feel that God can't handle your anger, depression, anxiety, disillusionment, lust, greed, envy, jealousy, hatred, confusion, frustration, loneliness, fear, sadness or suffering?

Many people report an increased feeling of intimacy in prayer after going through counseling. They have learned to bare their souls and become emotionally honest with God. They come to believe that God cares for them and wills their highest good.

The *Catechism* speaks of God as loving, generous, and desirous of communicating with his children:

> God's very being is love. By sending his only Son and the Spirit of Love in the fullness of time, God has revealed his innermost secret: God himself is an eternal exchange of love, Father, Son, and Holy Spirit, and he has destined us to share in that exchange (n. 221).[14]

A wholesome image of God empowers counselees to feel deeply loved by the Triune God. They discover that God is faithful in guiding their personality transformation and blessing them in all of their affairs.

Twelve

The Art of Counseling

I was recently interviewed for a program on "The Art of Counseling." Here are some of the questions and answers.

How have you lasted doing twenty-five thousand hours of counseling?

I've found counseling a satisfying but stressful profession because counselors listen to the very worst that can happen to people. We can't help but internalize some of their pain and suffering. I've burned out twice during my career. The first time I'd been counseling for five years. I scheduled too many people with too little renewal. The next time was fifteen years later when I had a major personal crisis. Both times I took a six month break for healing and the rekindling of my sense of mission.

I've learned that I can handle only so many people per week. This varies from counselor to counselor, but for me the number is about ten. That leaves me time to write, rest and play.

I believe that every counselor needs a strong hobby, avocation or friendship that brings renewal. My most special relationship is with my wife Katie, who edits my books. We go dancing, travel and keep our love alive. My hobby is weight-lifting at the spa, which regularly releases the tension I store up from counseling. I also read novels to give my mind a break.

Are there counselees who rub you the wrong way?

I don't have much patience for people who come to see me but don't really want counseling. When people are sent to me by the court or come in to blame others for their problems, I quickly force their hand. I make it clear that I don't have a need to counsel them.

This is different from my early days of counseling when I felt a need to help everyone. I guess I learned the hard way that a lot of suffering people don't want to change their ways.

How do you handle their lack of motivation?

I explain to them that undergoing counseling is challenging because it requires baring one's soul. I say that if they are willing to let me be honest in describing their resistances, then we can continue. But if they don't want my professional input, then there's no use wasting their time and money.

What are transference and counter-transference and how do you handle them?

Every counselee transfers their perception about the most emotionally significant person in their lives—usually a Mom or Dad—onto the counselor. This is called transference.

Let's say a man had an angry father who humiliated him all the time. He's going to expect the same treatment from me. He can't help this because it is unconscious. But I can help him by warning him in a second or third session that he's going to start feeling this way. Then the first time that he believes I've become angry with him or said something to humiliate him, I point out that I'm different from his father. Once counselees recognize their transference and work it through, they are freed from projecting their inner parent onto others.

Occasionally someone pushes my button by reminding me of another person with whom I've had a bad encounter. This is called counter-transference and means that the counselor does the unconscious transferring of a past relationship onto a counselee. When this happens to me, I try to become aware of it as soon as possible and then talk it over with another therapist. If I can get free of the feeling of counter-transference, I'll continue working with the counselee. But if I can't, then I'll refer the counselee to a therapist colleague early on in counseling.

In the event of a referral, I'd say something like, "My colleague is more skilled at handling your particular problem than I am. With your permission, I'll bring him (or her) up to speed and you can continue with him (or her) starting next week."

What if the person feels hurt or rejected?

This has happened to me twice and both times I agreed to keep seeing the person. The fact that we had openly discussed some communication problems seemed to clear the air. I bonded with each person and the counseling worked out fine.

How do you pace a session? How do you balance control with spontaneity?

This question has a paradoxical answer. I'm in control and I'm not in control. I prepare for the session with prayer and a quick review of past notes. Then I relax my body when a counselee comes in. I ask how the week has gone and how they are putting into action what they've learned. This warm-up phase lasts about ten minutes.

Next I probe to find out where their energy is. By this I

mean that their unconscious will know what they need to talk about. It may be a past trauma, a current dilemma or a future situation they are going to face. I listen until a concrete problem surfaces. I want something we can sink our teeth into, something that will create growth stretches in their personality functioning.

As soon as I can identify what this is, I move into the action phase of the session, where I suggest techniques. These include role-playing, muscle melting, anger ventilation, emotional catharsis or other procedures that move people forward. This working phase of a session lasts about thirty minutes.

The last phase takes about ten minutes. It is called getting closure and involves discussing and consolidating what they've learned. I prepare them for the week ahead by assigning homework that keeps them on a growing edge. Finally, I will them courage. By this I mean that I affirm that they are growing and changing in positive ways.

Regarding the question of control versus spontaneity in a session: as the counselor I'm always in control—like a lifeguard is in control of a swimming pool—but within that framework I allow a great deal of freedom of expression. This way counselees can guide me to their areas of deepest need.

Have you ever felt you were a failure with a counselee?

Yes. Over the course of my career I've made many mistakes. Several times I've pushed counselees too hard out of my own impatience and they've broken therapy. On other occasions I've gotten into power struggles, especially with controlling or aggressive counselees. This is embarrassing because I should know better than to become exasperated. Yet, I'm only human. When this kind of thing has happened I've had to face it. Sometimes when I've talked it over with the counselees, our temporary conflict has resulted in a stronger therapeutic relationship.

How do you see compass counseling in relation to other approaches?

Compass counseling is not in competition with other approaches to counseling, whether contemporary or traditional. The principles of compass counseling are available to serve every mental health and pastoral worker who assists people in growth and change. These principles are applicable in education, church life, childrearing and psychiatry.

How do you experience God in counseling?

God is the reason I got into this field. I had been to a seminary and then earned a Masters degree in philosophy at another college. But I longed to make a difference in people's lives at a deeper level. I took off three months in which I prayed day and night for God's will. At the end of that time a voice spoke to me out loud and said, *Dan, I've called you to be my psychologist.*

Since that time over twenty-five years ago I've found that God is a very active force in my counseling. I pray for a few moments before I bring each counselee into my office. I ask the Father to make his will known to the person. I invite the Son to communicate his love during the session. I entreat the Holy Spirit to oversee the counseling process with his wisdom and power.

There's a Scripture passage that captures how I see my role as a counselor. St. Paul wrote:

> I planted, Apollos watered, but God gave the growth. So neither the one who plants nor the one who waters is anything, but only God who gives the growth. The one who plants and the one who waters have a common purpose...for we are God's servants, working together (1 Corinthians 3:6-9).

Whether I plant the seeds of a growing personality or water the seeds that someone else has planted doesn't matter.

The deeper issue is that God is working with my counselees long before I meet them and he will be guiding them long after they've forgotten me. My mission as a counselor is to give people my best available attention and skill, and trust God for the outcome.

Appendix I

Compass Theory and DSM-IV

The compass of the self locates the polarities of love and assertion, weakness and strength, as universal compass points of personality (LAWS). The theoretical underpinnings for this personality compass were derived from the collaborative work of Everett L. Shostrom and Dan Montgomery. (See *Handbook of Innovative Psychotherapies*[15] and *The Holy Spirit in Counseling*[16]).

This is not to oversimplify the complex nature of human beings. Many other qualities play an important role in shaping personality, such as masculinity and femininity, or extroversion and introversion. However, these four basic compass points of love and assertion, weakness and strength, provide a clear latitude and longitude for personality health.

The compass of the self and the LAWS are theoretical tools that clarify the *Diagnostic and Statistical Manual of Mental Disorders,* or DSM-IV.[17] This manual is used worldwide and affords counselors with a consensus for describing human behavioral dysfunction. DSM-IV provides a classification system for diagnosing counselees, but does not indicate how to facilitate growth and change.

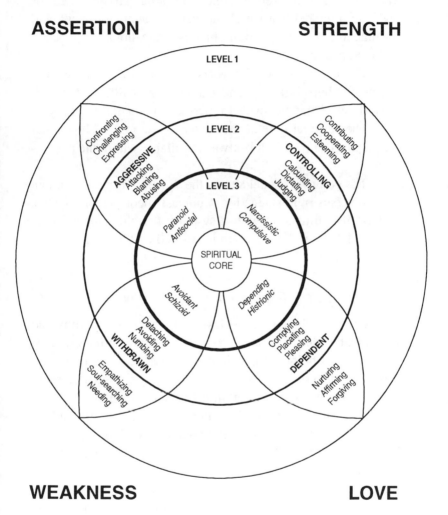

ASSERTION

STRENGTH

LEVEL 1

LEVEL 2

Confronting
Challenging
Expressing

AGGRESSIVE
Attacking
Blaming
Abusing

Contributing
Cooperating
Esteeming

CONTROLLING
Calculating
Dictating
Judging

LEVEL 3

Paranoid
Antisocial

Narcissistic
Compulsive

SPIRITUAL
CORE

Avoidant
Schizoid

Depending
Histrionic

Detaching
Avoiding
Numbing

WITHDRAWN

Complying
Placating
Pleasing

DEPENDENT

Empathizing
Soul-searching
Needing

Nurturing
Affirming
Forgiving

WEAKNESS

LOVE

THE COMPASS MODEL

The compass model organizes the major personality disorders of DSM-IV within the context of healthy functioning. The compass of the self responds to a long-standing need for one central model that simultaneously accounts for health and dysfunction. Compass counseling is educational, diagnostic and therapeutic.

The compass model reveals a bridge of continuity between psychopathologies and personality health, and moves inward, reflecting the levels of increased behavioral rigidity.

The spiritual core at the center of the model shows that the inspired help of God is always available within the personality.

The compass model shows the dynamic range of human growth versus rigid stagnation. Compass theory incorporates a system of malfunction with a system of healthy functioning. The model shows how growth is arrested and how growth can be restored.

Level 1: Healthy Expression

Level 1—the outermost level—describes the healthy and rhythmic balance of behavior available to all who integrate the four compass points of personality. In essence, the love point brings compassion for self and others, the assertion point brings courage to confront injustice and manipulation, the weakness point brings humility and empathy for others, and the strength point brings dignity and esteem of self and others.

The thin line of the outermost circle shows that the self boundary of a healthy person acts as a semipermeable membrane. This openness allows a two-way communication with others and God, resulting in identity, intimacy and community.

When people are balanced and healthy they express the inner core through direct behavior, as Jesus did. There is no pretense, masking or hidden agenda. We could call this being guileless and pure of heart. Also, input from others are taken to heart without the interference that defensiveness can bring.

Attitude-behaviors found in the outermost circle characterize compass living. These complementary opposites work to balance a person's personality and relationships. Compass counseling helps people experience greater wholeness.

Level 2: Partial Personality Patterns

Counselees generally exaggerate one or two of the compass points at the expense of the others. This one-sidedness leads to the Level 2 partial personality patterns known as dependency, aggression, withdrawal and control. My book *God and Your Personality* provides more information on these partial personality patterns.[18]

Counselees' inner pain congeals into rigid patterns of coping designed to ward off anxiety and to control life. Their compass becomes seriously skewed. They become prisoners of their own pride, defensiveness and fear. Wilhelm Reich calls this defensive posturing character armor;[19] Eric Berne calls it a negative life script;[20] Carl Rogers calls it an ideal self versus the real self;[21] Aaron Beck calls it an exaggerated process;[22] Jacobi Moreno calls it the loss of spontaneity and creativity;[23] Albert Ellis calls it a set of irrational assumptions.[24]

Partial personality patterns disrupt the fluid spontaneity of healthy personality. They contaminate and interfere with healthy perceptions of self, others and God. They arrest personality growth and cause stagnation.

Love deteriorates into pleasing, placating and complying. Assertion becomes blaming, attacking and abusing. Weakness contracts into detaching, avoiding and numbing. Strength is distorted into calculating, dictating and judging.

The circle around Level 2 is thicker than Level 1. This indicates that the rhythm and creativity of healthy personality has constricted into predictable and rigid behavior. Effective counseling reverses this rigidity, helping counselees to escape further deterioration into the downward spiral of dysfunction.

Level 3: Personality Disorders of DSM-IV

Personality disorders represent the severe rigidifying of personality into chronic, long-term patterns of behavior. Many psychologists today believe that personality disorders are highly resistant to therapeutic change. In contrast, compass theory holds that there is a bridge of continuity which connects pyschopathologies to personality health. The constricting downward spiral of psychopathology can be reversed into an upward spiral of personality expansion, conflict resolution and creative living.

The compass model makes it easy to understand the dynamics of eight of the DSM-IV personality disorders: the dependent, histrionic, paranoid, antisocial, avoidant, schizoid, narcissistic and compulsive.

Personality disorders are severely exaggerated distortions of the compass of the self. This is indicated by the thicker, more tightly constricted circle of Level 3. When the poles of personality are not integrated into complementary opposites, they become antagonistic forces that fragment the personality into warring camps. The poles that are avoided become unconscious and drive people to act out in self-defeating, repetitive ways. The poles that are over-exaggerated become frozen into character facades.

A character facade is defined as a counselee's presenting self or public self. A colloquial thematic word can describe the modus operandi of a character facade.

- dependent = clinging vine
- histrionic = prima donna

- paranoid = bully
- antisocial = con artist
- avoidant = wallflower
- schizoid = hermit
- narcissistic = big shot
- compulsive = perfectionist

Because every personality disorder can be located on the compass, a counselor can immediately recognize what perpetuates the personality disorder and what growth stretches will lead toward a balanced personality. The dependent and histrionic disorders are located on the love pole. The paranoid and antisocial disorders are found on the assertion pole. The avoidant and schizoid disorders are located on the weakness pole. The narcissistic and compulsive disorders are stuck on the strength pole.

Appropriate growth stretches awaken unconscious poles of the personality and gradually restore the full functioning of all four compass points.

Compass counseling reverses personality disorders by:

- educating counselees about what constitutes healthy personality and relationships;

- revealing partial personality patterns and discussing self-defeating outcomes;

- assisting people to make the unconscious more conscious and take responsibility for their lives;

- stimulating attitudinal and behavioral change by implementing techniques and growth stretches;

- developing in counselees a balanced perception of God and an intimate surrender to the guidance of the Holy Spirit from within their cores.

For an in-depth treatment of these personality disorders, I refer you to my book *Beauty in the Stone: How God Sculpts You into the Image of Christ.*[25]

Mixed Traits

The compass model helps pinpoint people's functioning, even if they exhibit mixed traits. We unravel mixed traits by breaking them down into their component parts. For instance, a controlling person with dependent traits will have a predominant need for perfection and a secondary need for constant reassurance.

In this case we work on growth stretches into the healthy dimensions of the weakness pole to balance out perfectionist control. Later, this can be followed by stretches into the assertion pole to balance out dependency. Gradually, the person exchanges the rigidity behind perfectionism and dependency for a more rhythmic personality.

Appendix II

The Globe of Human Nature

The globe of human nature integrates the four key elements of a human being into an overarching whole. Instead of overemphasizing thinking, feeling, sensing or spirituality, compass counseling says that the mind, heart, body and spirit are *all* important.

God created all aspects of human nature and wants to see them flourish. Counselees need to become more aware of the various aspects of themselves that they may have ignored or repressed. Maturity means a well-developed self.

Compass theory asserts that Jesus Christ came to affirm our human natures as he did his own. He valued the sensations of his body, the feelings of his heart, the perceptions of his mind and the guidance of the Holy Spirit. Jesus, the Son of God and the Son of Man, lived wholeheartedly without being hindered by a partially functioning human nature.

In the counseling process, God is invited to help counselees toward a recovery built upon all aspects of their natures. Compass counseling promotes the wisdom of a balanced foundation for living.

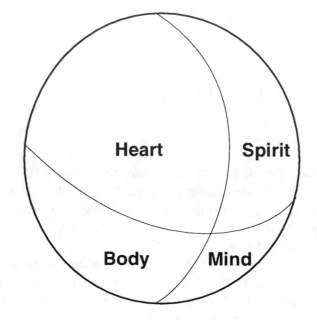

GLOBE OF HUMAN NATURE

A counselor looks for the most underdeveloped or overly exaggerated aspect of a person's nature and then suggests growth stretches to help bring about a balanced human nature over time.

The aim is to mobilize the most blocked aspect of a person's nature. When an impasse arises in counseling, usually the person is overly relying on one aspect of his or her nature. A mind-oriented counselee blocks counseling by intellectualizing everything. A feeling-oriented counselee throws up roadblocks by not engaging the mind. A body-oriented counselee is held captive to bodily appetites, but lacks development in thinking, feeling and prayer. A spiritually-oriented counselee may ignore emotions and bodily sensations.

The way through the counselee's particular impasse is to switch the therapeutic emphasis to the person's most avoided aspect. For instance, you would stimulate the feelings, sensations and spirituality of the person who lives in the head. You would stimulate the mind, heart and body of the person who emphasizes only the spirit.

By shifting the therapeutic focus to the least used aspect of the counselee's nature, you bring about growth stretches required for a balanced nature. You awaken and strengthen a vital contact with the whole nature.

Compass counseling promotes overall wholeness by utilizing a variety of cognitive, emotional, physical and spiritual techniques.

A Word to the Reader

I am an author who enjoys hearing from my readers. Writing is a lonely profession. I stare into the computer monitor for hundreds of hours, longing to see the facial reactions of those to whom I'm writing. Sometimes I wonder whether I'm making any contact at all, especially on the emotional level.

That's why I am so thrilled when people write and tell me how they felt about certain stories or passages, or how they responded when I disclosed my own struggles or triumphs. A dialogue between me and readers brings me great joy. I would like to hear how you have applied the principles in this book to your own ministry as a pastoral worker or counselor, and what has been the result. If you send me a photo, I'll tack it onto my bulletin board.

If you would like to know about my other books dealing with the compass of the self or compass counseling, please drop me a line. If you would like me to speak at a conference, retreat or church seminar, please write and I'll send you a resumé and list of workshops and speaking topics. If you would like to begin a *Compass Counselors' Group* in a church or mental health setting, turn the page and read the guidelines for doing so.

For now, thank you for reading *Practical Counseling Tools for Pastoral Workers.* I hope it has enriched your life.

Dr. Dan Montgomery
681 Portofino Lane
Foster City, CA 94404
415-354-8018

Starting a "Compass Counselors' Group"

Dear Leader,

Counselors and pastoral workers need creative ways to avoid burnout, remain spiritually inspired and enjoy stimulating fellowship with peers who know the rigors and joys of counseling.

Here are twelve suggestions for starting a *Compass Counselors' Group* book study in your city, parish or counseling center.

1. To develop people's interest, ask your local Christian bookstore manager to stock *Practical Counseling Tools for Pastoral Workers* for interested friends and colleagues. Also, you can order the book directly by calling:

Pauline Books & Media at 800-876-4463.

2. Phone or drop postcards to Catholic and Protestant therapists in your city. Drop a flyer to any group of professional religious. Contact professors of any nearby Christian colleges and universities who teach in the field of counseling. Communicate that you are beginning a *Compass Counselors' Group*.

List names and phone numbers of those interested. If you're already part of an existing staff, suggest that they adopt the book for a book study and peer support process over several months.

3. Set a starting date and overall timeframe. I suggest one hour per week until the book is completed.

4. Start each meeting with at least five minutes of prayer time. Let people pray silently or out loud for the presence of Christ to guide the group's progress.

5. The book study is carried on in a round-robin fashion. Each person reads three or so paragraphs, then shares personal experiences, needs and hopes. As the group leader, you are but a trusted servant, not a dictator or monopolizer. Let other counselors share (you may need to set an agreed-upon time limit of three to five minutes). Then invite the next reader to begin. If a person reads and wishes not to express a personal comment, he or she is free to do so.

6. Explain to members that there is no cross-talk, judgment or advice giving. Individuals are free to express personal experiences but must withhold comments about others. Stress the need for confidentiality, which is the lifeblood of trust and self-disclosure.

7. *Trust the group process and the presence of the Holy Spirit to draw people out and help them to be healed.* Develop a warm interpersonal climate free from moralizing.

8. Anything human is worthy of understanding. God accepts us as we are and desires us to become more real. Counselors are themselves healed and encouraged when they confide from the heart: "Confess your sins to one another, and pray for one another, so that you may be healed" (James 5:16). If a member tells another member what to do or not do, jump in with a gentle reminder that there should be no cross-talk, judgment or advice giving.

9. With ten minutes remaining, announce that only one or two more people can read or share. With five minutes left, ask everyone to mark the stopping point in the book. Stand up. Join hands. Invite someone to lead the Lord's Prayer.

10. Dismiss the group on time. Allow people to mill around.

11. When the book study has been completed, take a vote to see whether the group wishes to begin a new cycle at the beginning of the book. If so, let a new volunteer take over the servant/leader role. Pass on these guidelines to the new volunteer.

12. *Compass Counselors' Groups* can be open-ended and run year-round. Newcomers can join the group at any time and continue as long as they wish. The only criterion for membership is the desire for inspiration and support in your pastoral or counseling ministry.

God bless you and stay in touch,

Dan Montgomery, Ph.D.

End Notes

One

Compass Counseling

1. Adrian van Kaam, *In Search of Spiritual Identity* (Denville, NJ: Dimension Books, 1975), p. 7.

2. *Catechism of the Catholic Church* (Boston, MA: Pauline Books & Media, 1994), p. 238.

3. Eugene H. Peterson, *Five Smooth Stones for Pastoral Work* (Atlanta, GA: John Knox Press, 1980), p. 11.

Two

The Compass of the Self

4. Henri Nouwen, *Reaching Out: The Three Movements of the Spiritual Life* (New York: Doubleday, 1975), p. 12.

5. Richard P. McBrien, *Catholicism* (San Francisco: Harper Collins, 1981), pp. 1134-1135.

6. Adrian van Kaam, *The Woman at the Well* (New Jersey: Dimension Books, 1976), p.146.

Three

Compass Counseling in Action

7. *Catechism,* ibid, p. 566.

Four

Too Much Love

8. Rollo May, *Love and Will* (New York: W. W. Norton, 1969), p. 324.

Seven

Too Much Strength

9. Eugene Peterson, *The Message* (Colorado Springs, CO: NavPress, 1993), p. 31.

Nine

Getting Rid of Guilt

10. *Catechism,* ibid, p. 439.

11. *Catechism,* ibid, p. 365.

Ten

Dealing with Depression

12. Sidney Jourard, *The Transparent Self,* 2nd ed. (New York: Van Nostrand Co., 1971).

13. *Catechism,* ibid, p. 590.

Eleven

A Counselee's Image of God

14. *Catechism,* ibid, p. 60.

Appendix I

Compass Theory and DSM-IV

15. Raymond Corsini, ed., *Handbook of Innovative Psychotherapies* (New York: John Wiley & Sons, 1982), chapter one.

16. Marvin G. Gilbert and Raymond T. Brock, eds., *The Holy Spirit in Counseling,* Vol. 1: *Theology and Theory* (Peabody, MA: Hendrickson Publishers, 1985), chapter sixteen.

17. American Psychiatric Association, *Diagnostic and Statistical Manual of Mental Disorders,* 4th ed. (Washington,DC: 1994).

18. Dan Montgomery, *God and Your Personality* (Boston, MA: Pauline Books & Media, 1995).

19. Wilhelm Reich, *Character Analysis* (New York: Pocketbooks, 1980).

20. Eric Berne, *Games People Play* (New York: Grove Press, 1985).

21. Carl Rogers, *On Becoming a Person* (Boston: Houghton Mifflin, 1972).

22. Aaron Beck and Arthur Freeman, *Cognitive Therapy of Personality Disorders* (New York: The Guilford Press, 1990).

23. Jacobi Moreno, *Psychodrama*, Vol. 1, 4th ed. (Beacon, NY: Beacon House, 1972).

24. Albert Ellis and Robert Harper, *A New Guide to Rational Living* (Englewood Cliffs, NJ: Prentice Hall, 1978).

25. Dan Montgomery, *Beauty in the Stone: How God Sculpts You into the Image of Christ* (Nashville, TN: Thomas Nelson Pub.), 1996.

 **BOOKS & MEDIA**

ALASKA
750 West 5th Ave., Anchorage, AK 99501; 907-272-8183

CALIFORNIA
3908 Sepulveda Blvd., Culver City, CA 90230; 310-397-8676
5945 Balboa Ave., San Diego, CA 92111; 619-565-9181
46 Geary Street, San Francisco, CA 94108; 415-781-5180

FLORIDA
145 S.W. 107th Ave., Miami, FL 33174; 305-559-6715

HAWAII
1143 Bishop Street, Honolulu, HI 96813; 808-521-2731

ILLINOIS
172 North Michigan Ave., Chicago, IL 60601; 312-346-4228

LOUISIANA
4403 Veterans Memorial Blvd., Metairie, LA 70006; 504-887-7631

MASSACHUSETTS
50 St. Paul's Ave., Jamaica Plain, Boston, MA 02130; 617-522-8911
Rte. 1, 885 Providence Hwy., Dedham, MA 02026; 617-326-5385

MISSOURI
9804 Watson Rd., St. Louis, MO 63126; 314-965-3512

NEW JERSEY
561 U.S. Route 1, Wick Plaza, Edison, NJ 08817; 908-572-1200

NEW YORK
150 East 52nd Street, New York, NY 10022; 212-754-1110
78 Fort Place, Staten Island, NY 10301; 718-447-5071

OHIO
2105 Ontario Street, Cleveland, OH 44115; 216-621-9427

PENNSYLVANIA
Northeast Shopping Center, 9171-A Roosevelt Blvd., Philadelphia, PA
19114; 215-676-9494

SOUTH CAROLINA
243 King Street, Charleston, SC 29401; 803-577-0175

TENNESSEE
4811 Poplar Ave., Memphis, TN 38117; 901-761-2987

TEXAS
114 Main Plaza, San Antonio, TX 78205; 210-224-8101

VIRGINIA
1025 King Street, Alexandria, VA 22314; 703-549-3806

CANADA
3022 Dufferin Street, Toronto, Ontario, Canada M6B 3T5; 416-781-9131